THE BEST KIT HOMES

THE BEST

KIT HOMES

Save Time and Money on Your Customized Dream House

Joanna Wissinger

Produced by The
Philip Lief Group, Inc.

Rodale Press, Emmaus, Pa.

CREDITS:
Produced by The Philip Lief Group, Inc., 319 East 52nd Street, New York, NY 10022
Project Editorial Director: Constance Jones
Research: Joe Pheifer
Design: The Sarabande Press
Thanks to Ray Wolf and Margaret Lydic Balitas for their help in making this project a success.

Library of Congress Cataloging-in-Publication Data

Wissinger, Joanna.
    The best kit homes.

    Includes index.
    1. Prefabricated houses.   2. House buying.
I. Title.
TH4819.P7W57   1987   693'.97   87–4327
ISBN 0–87857–690–8   hardcover
ISBN 0–87857–691–6   paperback

2   4   6   8   10   9   7   5   3   1   hardcover
2   4   6   8   10   9   7   5   3   1   paperback

CONTENTS

A BRIEF HISTORY
OF KIT HOMES

*K*it homes enjoy growing popularity today because the idea behind them is really quite simple. If every house represents the combination of a lot of smaller components, why not sell packages of pre-cut, numbered pieces which buyers can assemble into houses? Using kits, people can build the homes they want while saving a lot of the money, time, and trouble they might spend building a home the conventional way.

For the last three centuries, pre-cut houses have met unique housing needs. They have, in fact, proliferated wherever a need to build a lot of housing in a short period of time has occured—for instance, in times of colonization. By importing European-style houses to Asia, India, and Hawaii, 19th-Century missionaries brought their culture as well as their religion with them, for better or for worse. Many such houses were also shipped to California during the gold rush of 1849.

Until the early 20th Century, this house-building method—constructing the house, numbering its parts, taking it apart, and shipping it out to be reassembled elsewhere—was too expensive for mass consumption. But with the invention of the power tool, the technique came into its first full flower. Now able to manufacture houses inexpensively and in quantity, Sears and Roebuck and other mass merchandisers began selling house kits by mail. Sears released its first Modern Homes catalog in 1908, and by 1930 had sold 30,000 homes. Sears, however, was neither the first nor the only company to manufacture houses and sell them through catalogs, nor even the first to sell house plans—companies like Hodgson Homes, Alladin Homes, and Montgomery Ward had started selling homes as early as 1895. But Sears became the industry leader.

Sears didn't revolutionize home manufacturing. The methods it used to produce its ready-cut homes had been used in house manufacturing for some time. But the company applied new marketing techniques during a period of strong economic growth, and its homes met with tremendous success. Sears homes packages resembled today's pre-cut houses in their completeness. The 1908 catalog, *A Book of Modern Homes and Building Plans*, offered 22 styles priced between $650 and $2,500. The price included plans, specifications, and all materials—right down to the nails.

With Sears' mail-order service, ordering a house was as easy as ordering a radio or a dining room set. When customers visited a sales office, they could look over the latest catalog, perhaps walk through a model home, and select a design that suited their space needs, design sensibilities, and pocketbooks. Standard home models ranged in size from two to eight rooms, and in

A page from the 1924 Sears Modern Homes catalog, showing the Princeton model.

A THREE-ROOM HOUSE UP IN EIGHT HOURS

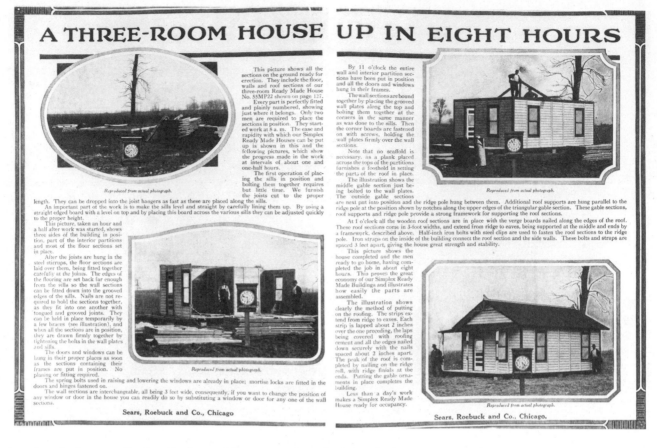

This picture shows all the sections on the ground ready for erection. They include the floor, walls and roof sections of our three-room Ready Made House No. 55MP22 shown on page 127.

Every part is perfectly fitted and plainly numbered, showing just where it belongs. Only two men are required to place the sections in position. They started work at 8 a. m. The ease and rapidity with which our Simplex Ready Made Houses can be put up is shown in this and the following pictures, which show the progress made in the work at intervals of about one and one-half hours.

The first operation of placing the sills in position and bolting them together requires but little time. We furnish the joists cut to the proper length. They can be dropped into the joist hangers as fast as these are placed along the sills.

An important part of the work is to make the sills level and straight by carefully lining them up. By using a straight edged board with a level on top and by placing this board across the various sills they can be adjusted quickly to the proper height.

This picture, taken an hour and a half after work was started, shows three sides of the building in position, part of the interior partitions and most of the floor sections set in place.

After the joists are hung in the steel stirrups, the floor sections are laid over them, being fitted together carefully at the joints. The edges of the flooring are set back far enough from the sills so the wall sections can be fitted down into the grooved edges of the sills. Nails are not required to hold the sections together, as they fit into one another with tongued and grooved joints. They can be held in place temporarily by a few braces (see illustration), and when all the sections are in position, they are drawn firmly together by tightening the bolts in the wall plates and sills.

The doors and windows can be hung in their proper places as soon as the sections containing their frames are put in position. No planing or fitting required.

The spring bolts used in raising and lowering the windows are already in place; mortise locks are fitted in the doors and hinges fastened on.

The wall sections are interchangeable, all being 3 feet wide, consequently, if you want to change the position of any window or door in the house you can readily do so by substituting a window or door for any one of the wall sections.

Sears, Roebuck and Co., Chicago

By 11 o'clock the entire wall and interior partition sections have been put in position and all the doors and windows hung in their frames.

The wall sections are bound together by placing the grooved wall plates along the top and bolting them together at the corners in the same manner as was done to the sills. Then the corner boards are fastened on with screws, holding the wall plates firmly over the wall sections.

Note that no scaffold is necessary, as a plank placed across the tops of the partitions furnishes a foothold in setting the parts of the roof in place.

The illustration shows the middle gable section just being bolted to the wall plates. The outside gable sections are next put into position and the ridge pole hung between them. Additional roof supports are hung parallel to the ridge pole at the position shown by notches along the upper edges of the triangular gable section. These gable sections, roof supports and ridge pole provide a strong framework for supporting the roof sections.

At 1 o'clock all the wooden roof sections are in place with the edges of the roof. These roof sections come in 3-foot widths, and extend from ridge to eaves, being supported at the middle and ends by a framework, described above. Half-inch iron bolts with steel clips are used to fasten the roof sections to the ridge pole. Iron straps on the inside of the building connect the roof section and the side walls. These bolts and straps are spaced 3 feet apart, giving the house great strength and stability.

This picture shows the house completed and the men ready to go home, having completed the job in about eight hours. This proves the great economy of our Simplex Ready Made Buildings and illustrates how easily the parts are assembled.

The illustration shows clearly the method of putting on the roofing. The strips extend from ridge to eaves. Each strip is lapped about 2 inches over the one preceding, the laps being covered with roofing cement and all the edges nailed down securely with the nails spaced about 2 inches apart. The peak of the roof is completed by nailing on the ridge roll, with ridge finials at the ends. Putting the gable ornaments in place completes the building.

Less than a day's work makes a Simplex Ready Made House ready for occupancy.

Sears, Roebuck and Co., Chicago.

A series of photographs details the rapid construction of a Sears home.

style from Colonial to Spanish. If they preferred, customers could even design their own homes and order the building materials from Sears.

Sears provided pre-cut lumber—a real advantage at a time when almost no one owned power tools—and complete specifications and construction guidelines for each house it sold. The construction manuals, some as long as 75 pages, gave detailed instructions to owners and contractors for every phase of building the house. Letters and numbers on the blueprints corresponded to those on the pre-cut lumber. With such complete instructions, buyers could, if they chose to, save money by doing some of the construction themselves. Assigned sales representatives made sure customers successfully completed their houses.

By 1933, however, the housing boom was over and the Great Depression was taking its toll. Sears managed to sustain sales until 1940, but then the slump forced it to discontinue its Modern Homes division. The company sold its lumber mill and ended production for good.

With the advent of World War II, the migration of workers to industrial centers to help with the war effort, as well as the mobilization of the armed forces, produced a demand for inexpensive, readily-available housing. Modern technology came to the rescue, and the war years saw the advent of panelized and sectional (modular) homes. The military in particular benefited from this new technology, which allowed it to set up bases and living quarters quickly. Manufactured structures proved invaluable even in sub-arctic regions, where the Quonset hut originated.

Rushed production, in combination with the shortage of many materials during the war, often resulted in shoddy construction, so manufactured housing developed something of a bad reputation. When the war ended and the country entered a period of booming prosperity, the market for pre-cut housing weakened. But in the 1960s, a number of demographic and cultural shifts fueled a revival in kit homes. New attitudes concerning architecture—which included a view of the

house as an assemblage of interchangeable parts—redeemed the manufactured house. Continued population growth, and the flight from the cities, created the need for more housing. And the growing interest in alternative life-

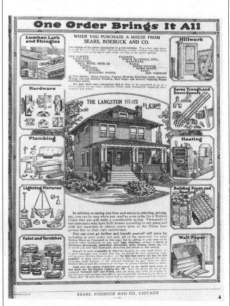

A page from the 1919 catalog lists all the materials provided for construction of a Sears home.

styles—in country living and in building one's own home—spurred an interest in all kinds of kit homes, including geodesic domes and log homes.

Kit housing has undergone even further change in the computer age. The Japanese make greatest use of computer technology, turning out manufactured houses the same way they make cars—with computerized robots. Approaching houses as they would any other mass-produced product, the Japanese carefully tailor them to specific market niches. In Japan, customers can design their own homes on a computer screen. Using the computerized design, manufacturers program robots to assemble modular houses which are 85% complete when they roll off the line. When operating at full speed, Japanese factories can complete a house every 44 minutes.

As a result of the cooperative efforts of the government and the housing industry, the Japanese have developed sophisticated technology virtually unavailable in the U.S. The application of such techniques as robotics and Computer-Assisted Design (CAD) means that, as yet, Japanese manufactured homes still cost as much as stick-built homes do in the U.S. But while the average Japanese house may cost $100,000 (compared with $50,000 in the U.S.), they offer many design options and interior features, and look just like custom-built homes.

Japanese manufacturers offer their customers enormous freedom of choice. At Sekisui, Japan's largest home producer, the customizing process begins in front of a computer terminal. Using CAD, potential buyers act as their own architects, choosing from among thousands of house designs and an equally large selection of materials and finishes. They can include household conveniences like a central computer that allows them to monitor the condition of their house, a

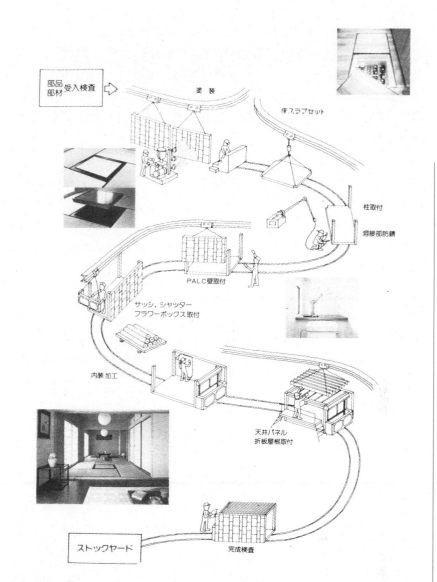

This diagram shows several stages in the construction of a Japanese home.

dining table that lowers into the floor, and space-saving combination toilet tank-sinks.

The computer responds to customers' design requests by displaying the customized house plans, and figures the effects of design changes on the total cost. If alterations push the price beyond the planned budget, another push of a button brings the standard plan back to the screen, and customers can seek new alternatives.

Once customers decide on their final plans, they and the manufacturer then agree on a production schedule and a completion date for the project. From framing to interior finishing, robots perform much of the manufacturing process. Then the completed house units are loaded onto a flatbed truck and delivered to the site, where a crane lifts them on to a waiting foundation.

Assembly of the units into a house takes about five hours.

As high technology plays an increasing role in everyday life in the U.S., American home manufacturers will no doubt adapt the Japanese approach for use in the domestic housing market. In the meantime, there's a whole world of kit homes to choose from. Providing customers an almost limitless choice of homes, from log cabins to sleek contemporaries to traditional colonials, the American manufactured housing industry continues to grow and change. In a world where busy working families expect the most out of life, the savings in time and money offered by kit homes make them the housing choice of more and more Americans each year. Kit homes are the wave of the future. ∎

CHOOSING & BUYING A KIT HOME

Many people dream of building their own home. For some, the perfect house might be a little New England saltbox; for others it's a rustic log home in the mountains. But whether they hope to own a rambling colonial or a spectacular contemporary, all hopeful homeowners encounter the same obstacle: trying to find enough time and money to build the home of their dreams. Prospective homeowners find that architects and general contractors often charge huge fees, that they're too busy to spend time building a house in the conventional way, and that tract homes don't offer the features or individuality they seek.

For those who won't settle for an ordinary house or pay more than they have planned for less than they want, kit homes offer a practical solution. Kit houses have come a long way from the "little boxes made of ticky-tacky" of the 1940s and 1950s. They now provide a rich variety of alternatives to conventional stick-built houses, and they even have some distinct advantages. In fact, many builders and developers use house kits in the most expensive subdivisions, and publications like *Professional Builder*, a leading journal of the home-building industry, often feature kit houses as solutions to problems of economy and quality.

THE ADVANTAGES OF A KIT HOME

A number of characteristics give kit homes an edge on conventional houses:

- Kit homes are less expensive than comparable stick-built homes.
- Because kit manufacturers maintain model homes for prospective customers to view, buyers know what their house will look like *before* they start construction.
- Kit home buyers can customize their houses to meet their specific needs. They can choose from a variety of features and interior and exterior plans instead of from a stock of pre-built houses.
- Kit homes are faster and easier to build than conventional homes.
- When they buy a package, kit home owners can add or eliminate features according to their budget. They can choose how much they will spend and know with a greater degree of certainty how much their home will cost.
- Because building a kit house involves less risk than building a conventional house, it is easier to secure financing for a kit house.
- Kit home buyers can participate in the construction of their home to whatever extent they want.
- Hundreds of manufacturers across the country offer thousands of standard house designs. Almost anyone can find a kit house they like, or have one custom-designed for less than it would cost to hire an architect.

FOUR STEPS TO BUYING A KIT HOME

There are four basic steps to choosing and buying a kit home:

1. Selecting a manufacturer
2. Designing the house
3. Calculating costs and finding financing
4. Construction

To be sure that they get the best value and the most enjoyment out of their kit home, those who decide to purchase one should pay careful attention to each of the four phases of the process.

1. CHOOSING A MANUFACTURER—BIG OR SMALL? Selecting the company from which to buy a kit house involves sifting through information on as many companies as practical to find those most likely to meet specific needs. Some manufacturers, for instance, specialize in houses with a particular look, while others build virtually any kind of homes their customers request. Kit home companies also differ in the types of construction they use—post and beam, panelized and modular, log and timber wall, geodesic dome, and metal houses each offer distinct features and advantages. Homebuyers should select the manufacturer that takes the approach best suited to their aesthetic and technical requirements.

Choosing a manufacturer, however, shouldn't depend on style alone. Buyer and seller establish a relationship over the course of the sale, customization, construction, and subsequent ownership of the house. Customers should buy from a compatible company.

While making the important financial and personal decisions that go along with buying a house, some people feel more comfortable dealing with smaller companies that offer highly personalized service. In the case of companies that produce a small number of homes each year, customers often deal directly with the president, who has a personal stake in seeing to it that customers receive the best possible service.

Some people, however, prefer the security of buying from a large company that has established a sound reputation by producing thousands of homes. Large companies can often offer price breaks because of the discounts they receive on raw materials purchased in bulk, and many maintain dealer networks that can provide assistance during and after construction. Dealers or other authorized representatives provide personalized service, serving as the link between the customer and the company.

Kit home buyers must also take manufacturer location into account when choosing whom to buy from. Some manufacturers ship only within certain geographical regions, but many ship nationwide. And while having a kit shipped across the country might add to the purchase price of their home, most customers willingly accept the extra expense to get a house that meets their needs exactly from a manufacturer that offers the services they want.

2. DESIGNING A KIT HOME—INTERIOR, EXTERIOR, AND ENERGY-EFFICIENT OPTIONS.

Kit home buyers rarely find exactly the house they want right in the manufacturer's catalog. In almost every case, they make some changes to dealers' standard plans, incorporating special options and customizing floorplans in order to come up with their own unique home. The ultimate design represents a careful balance of the customer's tastes, needs, and budget.

Kit home companies generally supply a portfolio of standard plans and design options from which customers can choose their basic house or find ideas for an entirely custom-designed home. Most companies maintain design staffs which work with buyers to modify standard plans or work up original plans. Customers usually pay a fee for this service. Sometimes the fee goes toward the final purchase price of the house, but even if it doesn't, kit home manufacturers charge much less for their design services than do architects.

Before making any design decisions, kit home buyers must arrive at an estimate of how much they can spend on their house. All of the choices they make regarding their house must stay in line with the planned budget. With a clear idea of what they can afford, they can then go on to plan their dream house.

Selecting the basic style of the house—contemporary or traditional, ranch or cape, tudor or mediterranean—is largely a matter of taste, although buyers need also to consider the demands of the climate and any limitations imposed by their site or local building codes. At this stage, kit home buyers must also determine how much

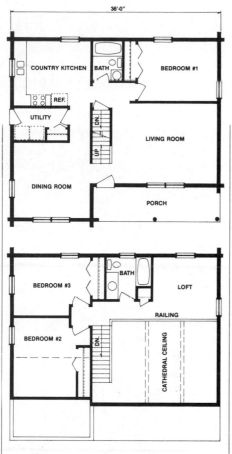

Kit homes can accommodate any number of design choices.

space they need. An evaluation of the space they currently live in and any planned changes in family size or lifestyle should give prospective homeowners a good idea of the amount of space and the type of layout they need in their new home.

With the basic requirements—exterior, price, and floorspace—in mind, customers can select the standard plan that most closely matches what they need. Buyers should remember that different manufacturers calculate floorspace in different ways—in some cases their figures refer to total enclosed area (including unheated space and storage areas with less than five feet of headroom), while in others they refer to heated living space only.

While many kit home buyers take the design process no further than indicating that they need three bedrooms and a patio, many others leave nothing to chance, and specify every detail of their house. Among the layout possibilities homebuyers will want to consider are:

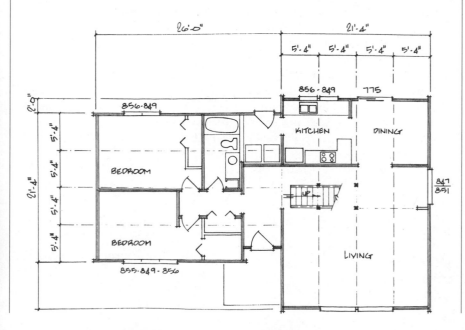

A wall panel under construction in the factory.

- Number and size of rooms
- Potential for future expansion — via additions or unfinished spaces (basements, lofts, etc.)
- Separation of living and sleeping spaces to minimize noise problems
- Location of master bedroom for maximum privacy
- Relation of kitchen to dining room for ease of serving
- Relation of kitchen to family/living/playrooms to make entertaining or minding children easier
- Eat-in kitchen
- Number, location, and types of bathrooms
- Special-use rooms: studies, workshops, exercise rooms, studios, etc.
- Lofts
- Separate laundry room
- Mudroom
- Front foyer
- Storage space
- Type and size of garage
- Number and location of entrances
- Direct entrance from garage

- Number, size, type, and placement of windows
- Skylights
- Special ceiling designs
- Fireplaces
- Decks, terraces, and porches

Once they have a floorplan for their house, kit buyers can choose interior and exterior details, like the type of siding and roofing they want to use, whether to use drywall or paneling on the interior, what kind of staircases they want, and the various hardware and trim details they'll need. Because manufacturers sell packages of varying completeness — some simply provide exterior walls, while others include everything down to the kitchen sink — kit home buyers make various types of interior design decisions in conjunction with their manufacturer's designers.

One of the most important design issues facing those planning to build a house is energy efficiency. Ever since the Arab oil embargo of 1974, neither homebuilders nor homeowners can af-

ford to ignore the cost of heating and cooling a house. Most manufacturers offer some passive solar or special insulation options, while some specialize in energy efficient houses that use either superinsulation, solar energy systems, or combinations of the two. Kit homes can accomodate all sorts of heating and insulation systems, and kit manufacturers offer a whole range of energy-saving items. Prospective homeowners need to master a specialized vocabulary and some new concepts in order to make the best decisions regarding the energy features of their house.

Good insulation contributes to energy efficiency by preventing the loss of heat through walls in the winter and by keeping summer heat from penetrating into the house. The various capacities of different insulations to do this are expressed in terms of R-values, which indicate resistance to the transfer of heat. The higher the R-value, the greater the ability of the material to insulate. Thicker layers of insulation provide higher R-values than thinner layers. Materials such as rigid foam and sprayed-on foam provide higher R-values when compared with conventional fiberglass batting.

For example, a wall constructed of 2×4 framing and insulated with 4-inch fiberglass has an R-value of 11 — more than twice as much insulating power as the same wall without fiberglass. A wall of 2×6 framing and R-19 fiberglass provides even greater energy efficiency, although it costs significantly more to build. By contrast, only 2.2 inches of rigid foam (such as Styrofoam) yield an R-value of 11. Of all currently available insulations, rigid and sprayed-on foams provide the highest R-values.

A number of kit home manufacturers offer "superinsulated" houses. Most solar house packages incorporate superinsulation to help make greatest use of energy captured from the sun. Along with a variety of other energy-efficient features, these houses have insulation on all six sides. Manufacturers generally use rigid foam to insulate these houses because of its superior insulating qualities. While superinsulated homes cost more to build, they offer the advantages of dramatically reduced heating bills and comfortable interior environments free of drafts and "hot spots."

When buying a superinsulated home, however, customers must take extra care to make sure their house has adequate ventilation. Because superinsulated houses are so "tight," they do not allow for air flow into and out of the interior spaces. Toxic or irritating substances can build up in the air if these houses are not adequately ventilated, resulting in an uncomfortable or even unhealthy atmosphere.

The total R-value of a wall depends on more than the insulation used. Every material used in building a wall can contribute to overall energy efficiency. Solid concrete offers an R-value of only .08 per inch of thickness, but plywood has 1.3 of R-value per inch. Wood has tremendous insulating value

due to its cellular structure, which includes lots of air spaces. Log and timber walls thus provide very high R-values that vary according to the species of wood used and the thickness of the walls.

Because the earth itself can serve as an excellent insulator, some house designs make use of a technique known as earth-sheltering. In this building method, builders bank earth around a house's basement walls and one or more windowless walls of the first floor, thereby insulating it quite effectively. The elimination of some windows contributes to this efficiency, because heat escapes easily through glass. Properly manufactured windows, however, can offset this problem. Double-glazing, triple-glazing, and storm windows (that create 1 to 4 inches of airspace between themselves and the other windows) can all prevent the loss of heat—and allow sunshine to warm the house.

Homebuilders should carefully seal insulation against moisture infiltration, because moisture can reduce by half the efficiency of insulation. Sealing tape at the joints and a housewrap of polyethylene can create a moisture-

Top: Dome homes can be quite lavish.

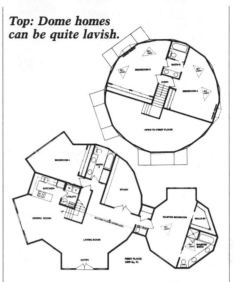

proof insulation envelope. Such a moisture/vapor barrier helps conserve the heat generated by a house's occupants, so that the house is not only warm but humid inside—great for plants, skin, and antique furniture.

The moisture/vapor barrier also helps prevent air infiltration, a major cause of heat loss. Wherever air infiltrates around doors, windows, fireplaces, and foundations—or even through the walls themselves—heat escapes. If structural elements are carefully fitted together during construction, builders can minimize the possibility of air infiltration. Foam caulking and weatherstripping around doors and windows also increase efficiency. Homeowners can also use airlock vestibules—double door systems—to prevent the loss of heat through open doors.

Solar heating systems have received a great deal of attention as a means of energy conservation, but many potential homeowners still think solar heating involves expensive, complicated, bulky equipment on the roof and in the basement. But of the two types of solar design—active and passive—only active requires collectors on the roof and a pumping system in the basement. Because the sun simply doesn't shine

Bottom: This home combines post and beam with standard stud construction.

A traditional log home makes a perfect vacation retreat.

enough in most areas of the United States, full active solar heating systems constitute a practical alternative for very few homeowners. In most cases, these systems provide only hot water to the households that use them—an important contribution, since hot water generally accounts for 30 percent of a home's total fuel bill.

A passive solar system, however, can provide as much as 90 percent of a household's energy needs—without all the machinery. With this type of system, the entire house acts as a solar collector. By orienting the house on its site for optimum southern exposure, and by using a lot of glass on the house's southern face, homeowners can make maximum use of sunlight to warm their house. Additionally, they can plant deciduous trees and incorporate roof overhangs to block sun in the summer and let it through in the winter. And they can design interiors so that air circulates freely, and the rooms used most frequently receive the most direct sunlight.

In passive solar design, a house absorbs heat from the sun into its walls, roofs, or interior spaces (via windows), and stores it. Heat stored in walls and floors radiates out into cooler airspaces, then air circulation takes the heat to all the rooms of the house. As the heat rises it warms the upper floors. There are three types of passive solar systems—each of which collects heat in a different way.

The first, and simplest, passive solar heating system is the direct gain system. Direct gain houses feature lots of south-facing glass and a thermal mass—a concrete block, often under the floor. Sun streams through the windows during the day, and the thermal mass absorbs it. When the airspace cools down, the thermal mass slowly releases the stored heat.

The second type of passive solar design, indirect gain, locates the thermal mass directly behind the south-facing windows. The thermal mass takes the form of a Trombe wall—a concrete wall, often painted black to enhance absorption, with vents for air circulation. The wall absorbs heat, which rises inside the wall and goes out through vents at the top of the wall. Vents at the bottom of the wall draw in cool air to be warmed. In addition to the action of the vent system, the wall itself serves as a thermal mass which releases heat gradually.

Isolated gain systems, the third type of passive solar design, use a separate room with many windows—referred to as a sunspace, solarium, or sunroom—as a heat collector. Heat collects in the thermal mass of the solarium floor, and then circulates to the rest of the house via blowers or fans.

Many kit home manufacturers offer passive solar packages that incorporate one or more of these systems, and some also offer active solar options. Prospective homeowners should consider their energy needs and the characteristics of their site and local climate when designing their homes. By planning for greatest energy efficiency, they can save significant sums on heating their kit homes.

3. CALCULATING COSTS, FINDING THE RIGHT FINANCING, AND ARRANGING PAYMENT. Once the kit home buyer has decided on design, the manufacturer draws up plans, completes a materials and specifications list, and calculates a price for the kit. Many companies also furnish budget estimates.

Customers can estimate the final cost of their completed house by determining just what the purchase price of their kit includes and what they will have to buy separately. Some manufacturers provide nothing more than the materials to construct the exterior wall system, while others provide turnkey homes virtually ready to move into. Kit home buyers should figure out exactly what materials they will need to obtain independently, and get a firm idea of how much those will cost. Using the plans and instructions provided by the manufacturer, homeowners must also solicit bids from contractors.

Based on their research, kit home buyers can calculate how much they will actually have to spend to finish their house. Most manufacturers estimate that the finish cost of a kit house runs two and a half to three times the cost of the kit itself. Those who serve as their own contractor can save 10 to 15 percent on this total.

When they know how much their house will cost, homeowners need to find financing. Most kit home buyers find financing more easily than those who choose to build conventional homes, because kit homes eliminate some of the risk and uncertainty involved in constructing a stick-built home. Many manufacturers have established good reputations, so loan officers feel better about financing their customers. Some manufacturers have relationships with lending institutions or can advise customers on sources of financing. Some even provide financing themselves.

Kit home buyers work out financing as customized as the houses they buy. Once they've found the money they need, they can make the down payment on their house. The majority of manufacturers require payment of 10 to 50 percent of the total price before shipment, and most will ask for some portion of that before they begin production of the house in their factory. Customers can sometimes get discounts by paying cash or by paying in one lump sum instead of in installments. When the manufacturer receives its down payment, it will agree with the buyer on a definite date of delivery.

4. CONSTRUCTION. Kit homes go up more quickly and easily than conventional homes, resulting in savings of not only time and energy, but of money as well. Some kits require the use of heavy machinery and others of specialized labor, but owners—even those with no construction experience—can get involved in the construction of any kit home to a greater or lesser extent. Those who buy kit homes often do so for this reason. They want to participate in the construction of their home, both because they can save money by doing so, and because it can be tremendously rewarding.

In addition to the savings they enjoy simply by buying a kit instead of building a conventional house, kit home owners can save anywhere from fifteen to twenty percent on construction costs by serving as their own general contractor. Though owner-contracting might appear difficult, almost anyone can do it if they pay attention to details and hire the right subcontractors. And kit home buyers have an advantage, in that most manufacturers provide some level of construction assistance. For those with the time and the inclination, owner-contracting can prove highly satisfying.

Those who participate in the construction of their own house—whether they do everything themselves or just finish the interior trim—save money, get exactly what they want, and gain a sense of pride. Kit homes provide the ideal opportunity for those who dream of building their own home.

COMPARING KITS— QUESTIONS TO ASK

Kit home buyers are more likely to be satisfied with their purchases if they ask a lot of questions *before* they buy. In addition to questions about the contents of a house package, customers can find out a lot about their potential homes by asking a number of questions of the manufacturer, its previous customers, and contractors who have worked on the manufacturer's houses. Manufacturers should willingly answer the following questions, or supply the names and addresses of current owners or contractors who can.

- How easy is the house to build? The best way to find out about this is to get the impressions of contractors who have built houses from the manufacturer's kits.
- How energy-efficient is the house? Buyers should ask the manufacturer for energy studies, and ask current owners about their energy costs.
- How much maintenance does the house require? Buyers can get an idea of how much work their house will be by asking current owners how much time and money they devote to maintaining their homes.
- What kind of warranties are there on the house, and who backs them up? Does the manufacturer guarantee the whole package, or are components guaranteed individually by their manufacturers?
- Are all of the materials used in the kit approved by state and federal environmental protection agencies for use in all states?
- How have previous buyers financed their homes? Buyers can learn about their financial options by talking to current owners or banks with which the manufacturer has financing agreements.
- What are the resale values of similar houses by the manufacturer? To find out how the value of their house might change, buyers should speak with previous owners who have sold their houses or check in the local registry of deeds for the sale prices of homes by the manufacturer. ■

A crane lowers panels into place to complete this home in a matter of hours.

COMPARING KITS—
A MATERIALS CHECKLIST

When choosing and buying a kit home, customers must keep in mind that each manufacturer includes a different mix of materials in its packages. Some log home companies, for instance, supply only the logs to build the exterior walls of a house, while some modular home companies provide houses complete in almost every detail—right down to the wall-paper. In addition, the standard price for a kit from one manufacturer might include the costs of such services as design modification and on-site technical assistance, while other companies might charge for such services.

In order to make a meaningful comparison of house packages, therefore, kit home buyers should thoroughly evaluate what each kit includes. The checklist below provides a complete breakdown of everything a kit home package might contain. Buyers should make copies of this list and bring it with them when they meet with manufacturers. By completing the checklist for each kit they are considering, kit home buyers can find out how the houses stack up against each other—and which provides the best value. ∎

ITEM	TYPE & MATERIAL	MANUFACTURER	GRADE/SIZE/ THICKNESS	NUMBER
Excavation and Site Preparation				
Foundation				
Footings				
Walls				
Floors				
Waterproofing				
Columns				
Basement entrance area				
Floor Framing				
Sill sealer				
Joists and headers				
Bridging, blocking, and anchors				
Double joists and headers at openings				
Subflooring				
Ceiling Framing				
Joists and headers				
Bridging and blocking				
Wall Framing				
Plates				
Studs				
Headers				
Rough sills				
Blocking				
Corner bracing				
Top plate				
Non-bearing interior walls				
Bearing interior walls				
Roof Framing				
Gable end treatment				
Dormers				
Overhangs				
Roofing				
Sheathing				
Underlayment				
Caulking				
Flashing				
Shingles or other				
Soffits				
Vents				

INCLUDED (YES/NO)	INSTALLED (YES/NO)	BONDING — NAIL, GLUE, ETC. (INCLUDE NAIL SIZE & SPACING)	IF NOT INCLUDED & INSTALLED, ADDITIONAL COST	SUPPLIER/ CONTRACTOR

ITEM	TYPE & MATERIAL	MANUFACTURER	GRADE/SIZE/ THICKNESS	NUMBER
Gutters & Downspouts				
Gutters				
Downspouts				
Splash blocks				
Exterior Walls				
Sheathing				
Underlayment				
Caulking				
Flashing				
Siding				
Windows				
First floor				
Second floor				
Sliding glass doors				
Skylights				
Basement				
Attic				
Exterior Doors				
Main entrance				
Other entrances				
Plumbing				
Hot water pipes				
Cold water pipes				
Waste pipes				
Storage tank				
Cleanouts				
Shut-off valves				
Hook-up to water supply				
Hook-up to sewer				
Hook-ups for appliances:				
Washer				
Disposal				
Dishwasher				
Refrigerator				
Outside hose hook-ups				
Vents				
Plumbing Fixtures				
Sinks				
Toilets				
Bathtubs				
Showers				
Electrical				
Wiring				
Panel				
Standard outlets				
Special outlets				
Switches				
Intercom wiring				
Electrical				
Telephone wiring				
Cable TV wiring				
Lighting fixtures				

INCLUDED (YES/NO)	INSTALLED (YES/NO)	BONDING — NAIL, GLUE, ETC. (INCLUDE NAIL SIZE & SPACING)	IF NOT INCLUDED & INSTALLED, ADDITIONAL COST	SUPPLIER/ CONTRACTOR

ITEM	TYPE & MATERIAL	MANUFACTURER	GRADE/SIZE/ THICKNESS	NUMBER
Heating				
Furnace				
Radiators				
Duct system				
Chimneys & Flues				
Chimneys				
Flues				
Flue linings				
Cleanout				
Fireplaces & Wood Stoves				
Facing				
Lining				
Hearth				
Mantel				
Circulation				
Insulation				
Exterior walls				
Foundation wall				
Foundation floor				
Floors				
Roof				
Interior walls				
Building wrap				
Vapor barrier				
Interior Walls & Ceilings				
Wall sheathing				
Wall tape and putty				
Ceiling sheathing				
Ceiling tape and putty				
Stairs				
Main staircase				
Treads				
Risers				
Stringers				
Handrails				
Balusters				
Basement stairs				
Attic stairs				
Finish Flooring				
Wood				
Carpet				
Tile				
Other				
Finishing				
Floor stain				
Floor sealant				
Paint				
Paneling				
Wallpaper				
Moldings				
Interior doors				
Closet doors				

INCLUDED (YES/NO)	INSTALLED (YES/NO)	BONDING—NAIL, GLUE, ETC. (INCLUDE NAIL SIZE & SPACING)	IF NOT INCLUDED & INSTALLED, ADDITIONAL COST	SUPPLIER/ CONTRACTOR

ITEM	TYPE & MATERIAL	MANUFACTURER	GRADE/SIZE/ THICKNESS	NUMBER
Finishing, cont.				
Casings				
Hardware				
Locksets				
Medicine cabinets				
Kitchen cabinets				
Other built-in cabinets				
Bathroom tile				
Other				
Additions				
Garage				
Decks, porches, etc.				
Greenhouses and sunspaces				
Other				
Plans & Planning				
Design services				
Blueprints and drawings				
Freight Charges				
Basic kit				
Kit items not delivered by manufacturer				
Other supplies to be delivered				
Forklift for unloading				
Crane for unloading				
Construction Assistance				
By phone				
On-site				
Labor				
Consultation				
Total Cost of Kit				
Cost of basic kit from manufacturer				
Cost of additional items from manufacturer				
Cost of supplies from other sources				
Cost of labor from other sources				
Total Estimated Cost of Finished Home				

NOTES

INCLUDED (YES/NO)	INSTALLED (YES/NO)	BONDING — NAIL, GLUE, ETC. (INCLUDE NAIL SIZE & SPACING)	IF NOT INCLUDED & INSTALLED, ADDITIONAL COST	SUPPLIER/ CONTRACTOR

POST AND BEAM HOMES

Post and beam houses use one of the oldest methods of building construction. Many of the early farmhouses and peasant cottages of Europe were built in this way, with frames of heavy, solid timber filled in with plaster and stucco. During the westward expansion of the United States in the nineteenth century, many homeowners abandoned post and beam construction in favor of the more quickly built "balloon" frame method, which uses planking nailed over a light wooden frame, and has load-bearing interior walls. With modern prefabricated technology, post and beam homes again became popular.

Post and beam framing uses timbers larger and sturdier than the conventional 2×4 studs found in other designs, with structural members spread farther apart than the common 16 to 24 inches. In contrast to partitions used in conventional stud-framed designs, the interior walls do not need to support the structure, so the homeowner has complete freedom in planning the living spaces. Windows and exterior doors will fit almost anywhere, if placement does not interfere with a framing member. This inherent flexibility makes post and beam houses extremely popular.

Flexibility extends to the overall house dimensions, as well. A line of upright posts—spaced at 8-foot intervals along the centerline of the building—acts as the "spine." Parallel to the centerline, rows of posts create the framework for the exterior walls. From the spine, the horizontal beams act like ribs, and meet the wall posts. The vertical posts support the roof beams, and this framing holds up the entire building. To increase the length of a house, designers simply add posts and beams. Longer beams make the house wider.

Designers can adjust much more than the length and width of the house. Adding height to the centerline beams results in a more steeply pitched roof. Eliminating the second floor creates cathedral ceilings and dramatic double-height structures, which can be accented by optional interior balconies. Raising one portion of the roof and inserting clerestory windows provides additional light and space. And homeowners can easily add wings to the structure.

Although these houses derive their structural system from the most utilitarian type of architecture, they have a strikingly contemporary look, frequently featuring large areas of glass

and open-plan interiors. Exposed rafters lend a warm appearance, rather than the cool functionalism frequently associated with modern designs.

These houses have a definite "look." Post and beam manufacturers do offer a wide variety of exterior styles, but a prospective owner can easily tell a Yankee Barn House from a Deck House, or a model from Pacific Frontier from one made by American Timber. No two houses share the same plan, or even the same silhouette. And post and beam construction means buyers can easily design the interiors of their homes to suit themselves.

Post and beam construction also results in a more energy-efficient house than conventional stud construction.

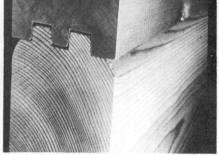

The walls and ceiling consist of a continuous "sandwich" of wallboard, insulation, and exterior sheathing, surrounding the structure with a "thermal envelope." This method leaves no weak spots or gaps where warm air can escape or cold air can enter, and the careful positioning of windows and doors can increase the heating and cooling savings even more. In addition, most manufacturers offer both active and passive solar design options.

The simplicity and ease of construction of these houses make them popular with do-it-yourselfers and the energy-conscious. ■

AMERICAN TIMBER HOMES

My husband, Richard, and I had planned to design and build our home ourselves," says Janet Osterbeck of Eagle, Michigan. "We started with a basement, then decided it would be too expensive, so we put the project on hold. Then we discovered kit homes. After quite a bit of research, we decided to buy a house kit from American Timber Homes and build it ourselves. We really liked the designs American Timber had to offer, especially the solar homes. Richard had designed our original plans—a south-facing passive solar house—and it was easy to adapt an American Timber design to suit us."

Based in Escanaba, Michigan, American Timber Homes manufactures a line of cedar houses that combines pre-built panelized walls with post and beam frames—in addition to a line of timber-wall houses. The company specializes in solar homes, offering both passive and active designs.

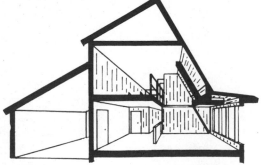

A cross-section of the Sun Wedge.

The company's houses feature many hand-crafted details that mass production techniques can't duplicate. American Timber's artisans create hand-hewn log trusses and similar items with tools such as axes, draw knives, and ship's augers. They make the trusses from uniformly tapered balsam fir trees harvested from the forests of Northern Michigan. First, workers peel the bark off with draw knives and stack the poles to season for as long as a year. Then a lumberjack uses an axe to hand-hew the poles to the desired shape. A finish lumberjack assembles the trusses, machining steel rings into the wood and hewing the poles to exact measurements.

Since the manufacturer saws, dries, and mills its own cedar, it can include hand-crafted details in its houses and still keep them affordable. It hauls timber from the cedar forests directly to the saw mill, cures it in the drying kilns, and processes it through the plant. The company harvests timber on a sustained-yield-basis—cutting no more than the amount that grows each year. The waste slabs and shavings from the sawmill and planing mill provide the fuel to run the kilns and heat the factory. This careful use of resources also helps to keep the prices lower.

American Timber Homes' active solar homes use banks of solar collectors to gather the sun's heat for hot water and space heating. Its passive solar homes use conventional water-heating systems, while south-facing windows bring the warmth of the sun inside for space heating. Storage systems in both designs hold the solar heat for release during the night hours and whenever the sun isn't shining.

The Galaxy model, designed by pioneering solar architect Donald Watson, has a steep-pitched roof covered with a bank of solar collectors, and a greenhouse addition that functions as a solarium. A balcony extending from the master bedroom out over the solarium allows the sun-warmed air to circulate freely throughout the house. The design requires a full basement to accommodate the solar equipment. In addition to the equipment, the basement provides space for a workshop or family room.

The aptly named Sun Wedge has a two-story slanting façade facing south and a bank of solar collectors. The roof slopes gently to a single story in the rear, and some models offer an attached one-story back wing. This design also makes

Top & bottom: Exposed beams, trusses, and timbers create American Timber's rugged country look.

an effective passive solar home. A garage shelters the house wall on the north. The Sun Wedge comes in a range of sizes, from 1,472 square feet to over 2,900 square feet.

Smaller designs for vacation, starter, and retirement dwellings average about 1,000 square feet. They range from the Cape Ann, a traditional saltbox design with a cathedral ceiling in the living room and master bedroom suite on the upper level, to the Keeweenaw, with a great room and a 14-foot vaulted ceiling. Other designs include a gambrel-roof model, a chalet, and a Bavarian-style home with an outside balcony projecting over the front entrance.

The Osterbecks liked working with American Timber because they could design their own interior. Their design has a split-level foyer that leads up to the main portion of the house and down to the lower level, situated partially below grade. "We paid $20,000 for the wall system, cedar siding, and roof truss," says Janet. "And then we bought our own roofing. We are very satisfied with the house—the materials provided were excellent."

Richard and Evelyn Crombie of Chardon, Ohio, also expressed satisfaction with their purchase. "We bought a kit from American Timber in 1980," says Richard. "It was the lowest-cost building option at the time, and it still is. We liked the idea of a kit home because we could build it ourselves. We also liked the energy-saving aspects of the design, and the high-quality materials provided. American Timber's wall panels are perfect and true, using very close tolerances. You have to put them up right. We paid $50,000 for a 2,000-square-foot con-temporary colonial house kit. It's a quality product, and I feel that we really got our money's worth. The house is so well insulated that it really almost qualifies as a super-insulated home."

While not difficult to construct, some American Timber models do require heavy machinery and a construction crew for certain steps. Most of the homes use the post and beam system; others, timber-wall construction. The panels for the first floor come in 8' × 10' sections, with the framing built in. As Richard notes, "They're pretty husky. You need at least six to eight people on your construction crew who are good at lifting to build some of these houses. With a two-story house, you really need to rent a crane to set the roof trusses. There's no way you could set them by hand. They're too heavy."

Putting heavy members into place doesn't necessarily take additional time. "We like American Timber Homes because we needed something that would go up fast, since we could only work on the house nights and weekends," says Janet Osterbeck. "Otherwise it would have taken forever. It only took two hours to put up the walls. My husband did most of the work himself, although he used a crane for the roof truss."

Prices for the basic kits range from about $20,000 to almost $100,000, depending on how much custom work American Timber Homes must do and whether the package is a closed shell or a complete home with interior finishing materials such as trim, doors, stairs, and paneling included. For example, a 1,040-square-foot Country Squire costs about $30,000 as a closed shell and about $4,000 more as a complete package. ■

A closed shell from American Timber includes:

- Exterior panelized wall with 2 × 6 framing, ½-inch sheathing, felt, treated Northern white cedar ¾-inch rough sawn vertical siding, and 6-inch fiberglass insulation
- Wood-framed windows, insulated, metal-clad, and pre-hung with hardware; and insulated wood-framed sliding glass patio doors with optional triple-glazing and vinyl cladding
- Roof package, including hand-hewn log trusses with dimensional timber trusses or brams with 2-inch wood roof deck (or conventional roof trusses with tongue and groove wood soffit material); insulated gables or gable frames with sheathing, lintels and 4 × 6 and 6 × 6 pilasters; laminated beams where needed, vent material for conventional roofs; and double cedar fascia
- Second-story floor system, with necessary joists, headers and hardware, plus ½-inch subfloor
- Interior wall framing with 2 × 4 and 2 × 6 studs and plates
- Porches and decks (where standard), with roof systems, treated 2-inch cedar porch deck, railings, trim, and steps
- All nails and spikes

The complete package includes everything supplied with the closed-shell package, plus:

- Interior doors, pre-hung, with hardware and trim
- Bifold closet doors with jambs, trim, and hardware
- Closet poles and shelf brackets
- Interior ¾-inch tongue and groove solid wood paneling, in choice of 8 woods
- Interior stairs with open or closed tread, matching balcony and loft railings, optional spiral stair
- Interior trim, including baseboards, window and door casings, and moldings for paneling and decked ceilings

The optional Vented Roof package for areas with heavy snow loads includes stripping and venting with special nails. The optional Sun Deck package includes Northern white cedar deck, skirting, railing, and steps. American Timber delivers the complete kit to the construction site.

The Homestead Dutch Colonial model combines a two-story gambrel-roofed main section with a single-story wing and garage.

29

BOW HOUSE

"T here is so much charm to this house," says Mimi Starke, a Bow House owner and the company's Eastern Pennsylvania sales representative. "The first time I saw one from the road, I knew it was for me. It was the first time I ever felt that there was anyone who understood what I wanted in a house. Bow House doesn't compromise—they don't stylize or offer synthetic substitutes for authentic details. It's all the real thing."

Bow House, a small company based in rural Bolton, Massachusetts, can't really be called a kit house "manufacturer" in the strictest sense of the word. Unlike other kit house companies, Bow House supplies designs and both interior and exterior details—rather than the bulk of construction materials, which the customer can usually purchase from local suppliers for less money. In this way, Bow House can ship the less bulky components of its kits to customers from coast to coast, and avoid the high cost of shipping huge quantities of lumber.

Bow House sells plans for authentic reproductions of eighteenth-century bowed-roof Cape Cod houses. This design has stood the test of centuries, and

A hand-forged butterfly hinge is just one of the architectural details furnished in the Bow House package.

A cozy interior results from the many details supplied with the house kit, including the mantel, hand-forged fireplace crane and eye, and custom-made hearth bricks.

has proved a most successful adaptation to harsh climates. Jack Rogers, founder and president of Bow House, puts it this way: "What we're trying to be is a better than average Colonial reproduction, put into a package. Although any carpenter-builder is technically capable of doing what we do, the detailing is too complicated for most of them. We do many, many custom things. People look at a Bow House and say, 'This is pre-fab?' Well, in a way it is."

What initially appeals to most Bow House owners is its uniquely curved roof. Sometimes called a "ship's bottom" roof for its resemblance to the keel of an upside-down ship, the curved roof has a practical as well as an aesthetic appeal. Bow House's twentieth-century innovation on the curved roof involves

Bow House supplies designs and both interior and exterior details—rather than the bulk of construction materials.

the use of laminated rafters for extra strength. The bowed roof also provides a great deal more shoulder and head room than conventional roofs, and on the second floor of the house it increases the amount of usable interior space by 20%. The roof also sheds snow well, an additional benefit in cold climates.

Throughout each of its models, Bow House combines historical details with modern technology, adapting eighteenth-century design to contemporary needs to achieve a blend of old and new. As Richard Gemp, a Bow House owner in Ridgefield, Connecticut, says, "I was attracted to Bow House because of the unique details—a good compromise between old and new. It was the size we wanted, and it had the authentic old details we love, but normal twentieth-century people could walk around inside without bumping their heads. I chose the house because of its blend of beauty, simplicity, and efficiency." Bow House strives to maintain historical accuracy without sacrificing comfort.

Jack Rogers founded Bow House when he realized that people everywhere—not

Top: Bow House creates an authentic Colonial ambience from details like special moldings and hand-blown glass.

Bottom: Nine-light windows, with their many small panes, are a historically correct detail.

Top: Typical floor plan for a full Cape.

Bottom: Hand-made pine doors have 1³/₄" panels.

just New Englanders—love the curved roof style. The Bow House product combines a partial kit with a design service. Bow House buyers get a package of unique, hard-to-find interior and exterior details selected especially for their custom house. They also get the services of Bow House architects and designers who work with them to design the homes they want.

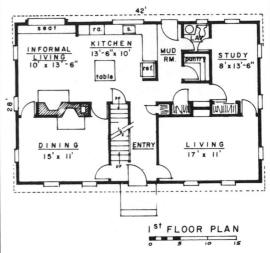

1st FLOOR PLAN

"I have problems with describing it as a kit," says Robert Ogle of Doylestown, Pennsylvania. "It's not like other kit houses, not in the true sense of the word. It's not a house that shows up on a flatbed truck and then you assemble it. It's more of an architectural and lumberyard experience—materials arrive in the raw, and you assemble them together. It's just like a custom-built house, really. Bow House is like a lumberyard that supplies the customized older materials that you could never find in a regular lumberyard. They'd be too expensive there."

Jack Rogers' fierce distaste for the standardization forced on homeowners by mass production motivates Bow House's strict attention to authenticity and detail. "If one hundred people build a Colonial house," he says, "ninety-nine out of that hundred will use the same newel post, because you are locked into what the lumberyards sell. They've got only one newel post, and everybody uses it—which is kind of a shame, because in the old days every one was different." Needless to say, all Bow Houses sport newel posts specially reproduced from

ones found in eighteenth-century Cape Cod houses.

Bow Houses come in four sizes, all steeped in Cape Cod tradition. The façade of a full Cape features two windows on each side of the front door. A three-quarter Cape has two windows on one side of the door, and one window on the other side. A half Cape has two windows to one side of the door, and a quarter Cape — the smallest of all — has only one window adjacent to the door. It looks like an enchanted doll's cottage.

The first stage in purchasing a Bow House, after reading the brochure, consists of sending away for a set of standard plans, for which the company will charge a fee. Customers can use the plans to consult with their local builder to determine the final costs of building on their site, and to decide what kind of budget they will need. When they give Bow House a non-refundable deposit of about $1,000, buyers may begin working with the design department to set up a construction program and put together the final plans.

Within the parameters of traditional Bow House design, the company is really very flexible. "You can do anything you want to as long as it looks like a Bow House from the street," says Jack. "That means no skylights on the front of the roof, but you can have them in the back. I have three unbreakable rules: no chimney on the end — it has to be a central chimney; no snap-in muntins on the casement windows — they have to be

A hearth with custom-made bricks, a beamed ceiling, and period furnishings make for a cozy kitchen.

A three-quarter Cape, with bowed roof in profile.

real; and no dormers on the front. What happens inside is up to you. After all, Bow House goes pretty far to make sure you have an authentic Colonial home. We do a lot of custom things. The back doors are handmade, and so is the divided-light casement window, because the colonists didn't have big panes of glass in their windows. The angled bricks in the fireplace have to be specially molded. We do all these things, throw a string around it, and call it a package."

"My wife and I previously lived in an eighteenth-century farmhouse that we renovated ourselves," says Robert Ogle. "When I talked to builders after we decided to build a new house, they were very inflexible about what they would and would not do and what kind of materials they would use. Bow House saved me from that kind of frustration. The whole Bow House experience was better than satisfactory—it was terrific. I

would go through the whole thing again tomorrow. We have a three-quarter Cape with what's called a Beverly jog in the back to accommodate the staircase and give us more space. In terms of customizing, there are certain parameters. You shouldn't violate the style. But otherwise it's really flexible."

Richard Gemp agrees. "We built a three-quarter Cape with four bedrooms

This half-Cape has a solarium addition at the back.

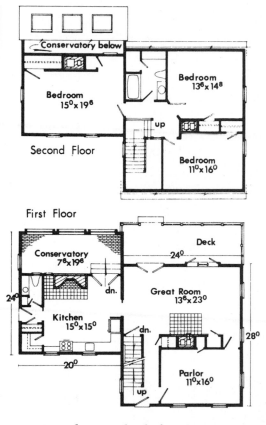

Second Floor

Bedroom
15⁰x19⁶

Conservatory below

Bedroom
13⁶x14⁸

up

Bedroom
11⁰x16⁰

First Floor

Conservatory
7⁶x19⁶

Deck
24⁰

dn.

Great Room
13⁶x23⁰

24⁰

Kitchen
15⁰x15⁰

dn.

28⁰

20⁰

Parlor
11⁰x16⁰

up

upstairs. The standard plan doesn't offer this, but we worked with the design people at Bow House to make changes. We swapped ideas around three or four times before we got the final version set. The final result is thirty feet deep and thirty-six feet wide, with an addition to accommodate a fourth bedroom upstairs and a laundry room downstairs. It's a basic house with great details. I think that the product Jack Rogers offers is terrific. He really cares what he puts on the market."

Jack Rogers explains the difference between Bow House and more conventional kit house producers in this way: "Bow House isn't saying, 'We'll save you money'—not compared to a straightforward house a good builder can build. But you are getting a house you could not ordinarily have. We're selling a house

with a particular style. You're buying a house for its appearance. You could build this house — anybody could build a Bow House. Technically, it's not difficult. But once you chase all these materials down, it ends up being much cheaper to buy the package. That's my function, to gather all the special materials together. It might cost you five thousand dollars more than an ordinary home, but it's thirty thousand dollars less than trying to do it all by yourself."

"The convenience of a packaged home was secondary as far as I was concerned," says Mimi Starke. "It's the design that I love. I've lived in my house since 1977, and it's been a wonderful experience. As a Bow House representative, I'm proud to show people my home. My husband and I collect Colonial-era antiques, and the house is a perfect place to show them off."

"The bowed roof catches your eye at first," says Richard Gemp. "The authentic details are like icing on the cake. I

Floor plan for the house on the previous page shows how the solarium fits into the scheme of things.

All hardware provided is hand-forged or custom-made.

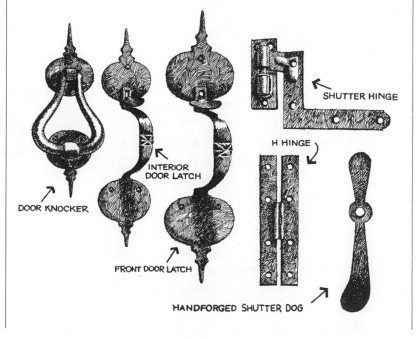

DOOR KNOCKER

INTERIOR DOOR LATCH

FRONT DOOR LATCH

SHUTTER HINGE

H HINGE

HANDFORGED SHUTTER DOG

like Colonial details, an older look as opposed to contemporary. When I moved my family to Connecticut from Illinois

---

"The bowed roof catches your eye at first," says a Bow House owner, *"And the authentic details are like icing on the cake."*

---

in 1981, there weren't a lot of houses available on the market. Originally, we didn't want to build a house—too expensive. But my wife and I couldn't find a house we both liked and could agree on buying. I had been carrying the Bow House brochure around for four or five years, and we finally decided to go ahead with it. Building the house was not difficult. It's not unique from a construction standpoint. Anybody who's built a house can build a Bow House. It's the details that are really special. It took the same amount of time to build as a conventional house, and might have cost a little bit more. But it's unique and a really neat house to live in—it really grows on you."

"This is a very small company," says Jack Rogers. "We put everything together in our factory, which is a former dairy barn, and ship house packages all over the country. Often, our customers are real purists, real Colonial nuts—

they conceal the appliances and fill the houses with antiques and really good reproductions so that it's as though you walked into the eighteenth century and nothing's changed since. Some people just like good design—the curve of the roof just appeals to some people. But the real focus is Colonialism."

"There's so much quality that goes into a Bow House," says Mimi. "They aren't very big, but bigger isn't necessarily better. It's got thoughtful design and a lot of aesthetic appeal—something really terrific in a small package. The

Bow House windows feature hand-blown glass, inch-thick casings, and authentic window pins.

people at Bow House are honest New England people. They work hard at what they do and they believe in their product. I think that's really something, these days."

Bow House works out a separate price for each package. For example, the cost of a standard 2,275-square-foot full Cape kit without custom modifications comes to $34,718—with the full price estimated at between $130,000 and $160,000, including allowances for site development, appliances, kitchen cabinets, and light fixtures. Plans and details for a modified 2,563-square-foot version of the same house cost $37,475. By contrast, a smaller house, such as the 1,182-square-foot quarter Cape, costs $20,232 in kit form and between $80,000 and $90,000 to complete. Bow House also sells auxiliary structures, such as solar greenhouses, garages, and garden structures. ■

A Bow House "Architectural Package" includes a building manual, and enough interior and exterior details so that the house *looks* like a Bow House. The components of this package include:

- □ **Laminated bowed roof rafters, pre-cut and shaped**
- □ **White cedar roofing shingles**
- □ **Cedar siding, interior and exterior trim**
- □ **Handmade 1³/₄-inch thick interior and exterior doors, with hardware**
- □ **Wide pine floor boards**
- □ **Stairs with railing, baluster, and newel post**
- □ **Fireplace mantel, with fireplace crane and eye**
- □ **"Beehive" attic register**

In short, the package contains enough details to ensure traditional Colonial construction. You can purchase other materials from local lumberyards, and additional finishing touches are available as options from Bow House.

A full Cape with a matching garage basks in the sun.

DECK HOUSE

*A*fter a year of looking for a vacation/rental home to buy in Florida, Carolyn Opar and her husband Michael decided to build when they couldn't find a pre-built house they liked. They had bought some land and begun thinking about the kinds of design and materials they wanted to include in the house, when they visited friends in Pennsylvania. "They'd built a Deck House," recalls Carolyn. "And the quality of the work and materials really impressed us. So we decided to try it for ourselves." Later, when they opted to find a new primary residence in Long Grove, Illinois, they again chose to build a Deck House "because we were so pleased with the Florida house," says Carolyn.

Deck Houses always seem to bring out this sort of enthusiasm in their owners. Since 1960, Deck House has produced a wide variety of home designs, including passive solar models. Not only does the company manufacture the pre-cut post and beam house package, it produces many of the components as well, using high-quality materials to make everything from mahogany staircase railings to laminated cedar decking to insulated windows and frames. Its practice of

This page:
Top: Outside, Deck House designs offer rugged styling and lots of windows.

Bottom: Interiors glow with exposed wood and plenty of sunlight.

Opposite page:
Top: Houses in the Conservatory Collection offer many solar features, such as this sunroom.

Bottom: A Deck House under construction reveals the integrity of the post and beam frame.

manufacturing such components results in lower total production costs — and reduced prices for its kits.

Every element of a Deck House makes use of superior materials like mahogany, brick, and stone, and each Deck House is distinguished by luxurious details like brass hardware, cedar paneling, and brick chimneys. The use of premium materials lends Deck Houses a rich, natural-hued look and the durability of

---

"The engineering and design are extraordinary," notes one Deck House owner. *"The house is straight and true and every line is plumb."*

---

homes meant to last for generations. Douglas Henry, another Deck House owner, feels that the company offers a product "very much like a custom house — or like a Cadillac or Mercedes. The materials are just superb." He goes on to relate that, while his house was under construction, "everyone was really impressed with the Deck House detailing." Deck House owners like Doug point to three features of Deck House detailing that they feel add an extra air of quality to their homes: mahogany millwork, brass and chrome hardware, and specially manufactured windows.

Deck House employs mahogany for a number of interior details, including staircases, railings, and balustrades, as well as baseboards, cove lighting, wall-mounted light fixtures, and covers for baseboard heaters. The company also crafts exterior doors—in a variety of designs—and screen/storm door frames from mahogany. Because of the wood's stability—its resistance to the shrinkage and expansion that can result from exposure to moisture—Deck House uses Philippine mahogany for its specialty millwork. This type of mahogany offers other advantages in that it can be worked easily and takes a fine finish. Eschewing the traditional treatment of the wood—which generally yields a dark, almost dreary finish—the company favors the use of two coats of preservative sealer in place of heavy layers of stain and lacquer. This technique brings out mahogany's natural warm brown.

To complement the rich tones of the mahogany and cedar used in its house interiors, Deck House offers a choice of chrome- or brass-finish door and window hardware. The company supplies everything from lever handles to friction hatches, and produces the frames and opening cranks for all doors, windows, sliding glass doors, and skylights in bronzetone. The company's efforts to ensure color harmony extend even to the spacers in the insulated glass it uses.

Deck House manufactures both the window frames and the insulated glass for its kits. The company makes the glass using a dual-seal method meant to minimize the chance of seal failures, and specially mills the mahogany window frames to match the houses' exteriors and coordinate with the overall Deck House look. Its precision-engineered windows include frames grooved to accommodate interior and exterior siding and channels that direct rainwater away to prevent leaks. And they're designed to eliminate the need for extra trim material—the trim is built right in.

Most Deck House owners follow an open plan when designing the interiors of their homes, because it shows off the lush wood surfaces to their best advantage. This type of design incorporates the liberal use of glass in window-walls and sliding glass doors, an approach the Opars took with both of their Deck Houses. They chose their Illinois home,

40

for example, from the company's Conservatory Collection, which features passive solar houses. According to Carolyn, "The south window wall, which is twenty feet high, contains glass from floor to ceiling."

The Opars designed their houses with the help of a Deck House designer, and found the whole process easy and enjoyable. "Since they're put together in eight-foot increments, Deck Houses are easy to plan. You just can't build a bad Deck House," states Carolyn. A distinct advantage of the post and beam construction was that it allowed the Opars to place interior walls wherever they wanted to. Carolyn describes how she and Michael went about planning their home in Illinois: "We're not architects, my husband and I, but the Deck House designers really helped us to get what we wanted. We sat down with a piece of paper and made a list of rooms, and then

we sketched a plan we thought we'd like. We took it to Deck House, and the designer laid it out for us and made a few changes, and we ended up with pretty much what we wanted.

"You know," she continues, "when you're building a house, there are certain things you want, there's a certain feeling you strive for in the house." What the Opars wanted —and got— was an unrestricted sense of space. Their open-plan downstairs includes a great room, living room, kitchen, and master bedroom suite, while upstairs, a loft containing two bedrooms looks out over the great room through an open hallway. The limited number of interior walls and the extensive use of glass brings the outdoors right into the house and gives the Opars a view of the surrounding woods from almost anywhere in the house. Features like this make the Opars very satisfied with both the process and results of customizing their Deck House. "Dealing with Deck House was great," exclaims Carolyn. "And we absolutely love the feeling of openness."

Deck House takes a system approach to producing quality kit homes, combin-

ing careful architectural design, meticulous component manufacturing, and precision-engineered construction. Doug Henry finds the results of this system to his liking: "The engineering is really incredible. All the subcontractors brought their families by to look at the house." Tongue and groove interlocking cedar decking, laminated for strength and nailed to the post and beam frame, forms the floor and roof and creates a handsome ceiling of exposed cedar. Wherever possible, Deck House replaces plastic, Sheetrock, and other synthetic building materials with wood, not only for its aesthetic appeal but for its structural strength.

The post and beam frame of a Deck House must be sturdy enough to hold up the entire house, because the interior walls aren't loadbearing. This provides for a great deal of versatility in interior design, as homeowners can place the interior walls without concern for the house's support requirements. Deck House uses laminated wood roof and floor beams, which are pound for pound stronger than steel. Because the company engineers its structural components with a margin of error of just $1/16$ inch, Deck House construction involves almost unparalleled precision.

Everything in a Deck House kit fits together exactly. For example, a bevel at the ridge end of each roof beam allows the beams to meet at exactly the correct angle, while a diagonal cut at the opposite end of each ensures that the beams rest securely on their supporting posts. Additionally, routed grooves in the beams create recesses into which the cedar siding fits snugly. Doug Henry appreciates Deck House's attention to de-

tail, and notes, "The engineering and design are extraordinary. The construction technique employs such exact dimensioning—it really has to be put together right. The house is straight and true and every line is plumb."

The post and beam frame of each Deck House supports walls no less painstakingly designed. The company strives to produce the most energy-efficient houses possible by focusing on careful wall construction and insulation. The tight fit of wall components with one another reduces the likelihood of air infiltration, the main cause of heat loss in residential structures. Deck House sheaths its wall panels in plywood specially cut to overlap the supporting posts between panels. Inside the walls, a continuous polyethylene sheet

Model 7163 incorporates a master bedroom suite with a private deck.

All home designs from Deck House include plenty of windows.

between the insulation and the interior wall surface acts as a barrier against moisture infiltration.

In addition to the attention it pays to wall construction, Deck House improves energy efficiency by carefully engineering components to fit together snugly. Beams and window sills, for example, have special grooves designed to produce an interlocking rather than butt joint between them. All exterior doors have heavy-duty weather stripping, and weather stripping on all sides seals against air leakage when wooden sash windows are securely latched. Window frames, milled to prevent cracks at their joints, include grooves that accommo-

date storm windows (as well as screens) and compression gaskets inserted where the frames meet beams and wall panels.

The precise design of Deck House construction involves a lot of attention to detail. For this reason, Deck House advises homeowners against trying to assemble their kits without professional help. Some Deck House owners, in the interest of saving about 10% on the total cost of their homes, act as their own contractors, as did Doug Henry. A military officer, Doug used his accumulated leave time to oversee construction. Though it took a lot of time and energy, Doug feels pleased by the results: "It's a beautiful house—it's well worth going

Clerestory windows, such as those shown here, bring light into the interior from above.

through the process of building your own house to get something like this."

Doug did all his own site preparation and foundation work, then hired a framing crew to do the actual construction. Because he had completed the seminar Deck House offers those who choose to act as their own contractors, he was able to show the framing crew what to do—and make sure they did things right. "Some points required a judgment call," he says, "and I decided what was to be done." Throughout the process, he had the security of knowing that he could call Deck House's toll-free number for help.

Because Deck House uses materials like mahogany and cedar, its kits are not inexpensive. But because of the economies of scale enjoyed by such a large manufacturer, Deck House buyers get premium materials and features at much lower prices than they would if they built independently. And many items included in a Deck House kit might prove very difficult to obtain from the local lumber store. But even with the savings that come with bulk purchasing, Deck Houses are among the more expensive kit homes.

Deck House prices each kit individually because each is custom designed and manufactured, but the company does provide price guidelines in its catalog. The company's estimates include not only the cost of the kit, but rough figures for the cost of construction, which includes site development, foundation work, labor, and mechanical systems. At the low end, a 1,581-square-foot kit runs from $85,000 to $105,000 completely finished; and at the high end, a 4,843-square-foot house ranges from $200,000

An interior balcony overlooks a sunny living room, a frequent Deck House design feature.

to $220,000. According to the Deck House estimates, Doug Henry's 3,400-square-foot model cost from $150,000 to $170,000, although he probably saved $15,000 to $17,000 by serving as his own general contractor. ∎

A Deck House kit contains:

- □ Post and beam structural system of Douglas fir beams
- □ Exterior wall panels
- □ Laminated cedar decking for walls, floors, and ceiling
- □ Rough-textured Western red cedar or Atlantic white cedar exterior siding, tongue and grooved for secure fit
- □ All insulation for walls, floors, and ceiling, plus a polyethylene moisture barrier
- □ All windows, with specially milled mahogany frames, distortion-free insulated glass, and hardware
- □ Mahogany interior and exterior doors, pre-hung in mahogany frames, with hardware
- □ All mahogany interior trim, including staircases, railings, balustrades, baseboards, and cove lighting

GREEN MOUNTAIN HOMES

This page:
Top: A spacious two-story custom design is also energy-efficient.

Bottom: Green Mountain Homes offers townhouse plans as well as single-family homes.

Opposite page: Post and beam construction adapts well to an open plan interior.

W ay back in the early seventies, during the energy crisis," reports Dr. John Lewis of Charlotte, Vermont, "I thought about how to make my own home energy efficient. I decided that the best way to go about it was the Roman hypocaust system, employing a thermal mass to retain heat and air ducts to circulate it, all located in the foundation. About ten years after this, when I found myself building a new home, I chose a kit from Green Mountain Homes because their designs employ the same system—better than I could do it myself."

Green Mountain Homes, based in Royalton, Vermont, manufactures kits in a variety of traditional home styles, including saltboxes, Cape Cods, and gambrel-roofed homes. Founded in 1975 by James and Cornclia Kachaturian, the company embraces a corporate philosophy of working with natural energies to improve the efficiency of their houses. All Green Mountain homes feature a patented solar-collection technology, based on direct-gain solar techniques.

The Solar Slab design incorporates a ground-floor heat exchanger and thermal-mass radiant floor design with a simple direct-gain collection system. During the day, air warmed by the sun is drawn down into the ducts in the concrete floor, where an air exchange sys-

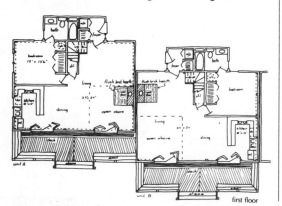

first floor

tem sends it out to the rest of the house. At night, the heat stored in the thermal slab radiates out to the rest of the house, maintaining an even interior temperature during the hours the sun doesn't shine.

"The heating system works," says John Lewis. "I heat my house for the winter with solar heat and three and a half or four cords of wood. I installed baseboard heating as a backup in two rooms with northern exposure and only used it once, when my eighty-five-year-old mother came to visit. We've left the house closed up in the winter for ten days to two weeks and had no problems. The lowest temperature the house ever reached when shut up like that was fifty-three degrees—and that was during a Vermont February!"

In addition to the Solar Slab system, Green Mountain homes include a number of other energy-efficient features. A multilayered Thermal-Break wall construction, which employs two layers of insulation separated by plywood sheathing and incorporates a moisture infiltration barrier, prevents stored heat from escaping. The interior portion of the wall, thermally isolated from the exterior part, makes it much harder for heat to escape. Insulated wooden Thermo-Shutters on the windows also help protect against heat loss.

"It's impressively simple and effective," says Harold Olsen, owner of a Green Mountain house in Woonsocket, Rhode Island. "There are no moving parts. We have been very comfortable during the two winters we've lived in this house. We chose Green Mountain because it had the best system. The house works very well—you do have to

Top: A solarium can supply extra heat from the sun.

Bottom: Solar homes can be elegant as well as efficient.

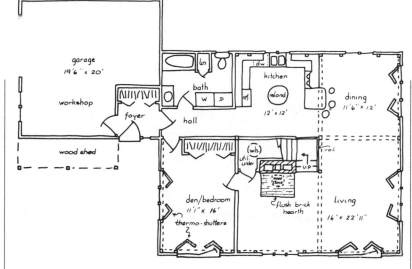

anticipate it a little, and get into the rhythm of remembering to open and close the windows and shutters at the right time. We have thermal shutters, which we open during the day to let in sunlight, and close at night to keep out the cold. In the summertime, it works the opposite way to keep the house cool. It's really just a question of attention to detail, since nothing works automatically. But it's very easy, for instance, to set the house up so you can go away and leave it in the winter and it stays at an even interior temperature. Even though we're not fanatics about conserving heat, the house stays warm.

"One day last winter, we accidentally shut off the gas furnace. We didn't realize what had happened for three or four

> "*I* enjoyed the experience of building this house so much I'd like to build another one."

days—we were quite comfortable with just the wood stove," Harold continues. "In a twelve-month period, our bills for heat, hot water, cooking, and so on, came to a total of six hundred dollars. We didn't use much wood either—only about half a cord."

The simple, straightforward exterior designs available for Green Mountain homes also appeal to customers. "We

liked the looks of the house, that's why we bought it," says Harold. "Once we saw the house we liked, we just wanted that house. We liked the Green Mountain house better than any stickbuilt house in the same price range. Jim Kachaturian has a good eye for how a house should look. We wanted a house that was distinctive and built to look like and to be what it is. This house is straightforward, neat and simple in its 'houseness.' I was nervous about a solar house because I didn't want too many gimmicks—no pipes on the roof or anything like that. But this house is great."

John Lewis feels the same way. "I had three reasons for building a kit house. One was that it had the heating system that I wanted. Secondly, I had the reassurance of knowing exactly what I would get for my money. Third, I saved money by getting the shell up rapidly. The post and beam frame makes designing the house very flexible. I appreciated being able to design my own interior. Green Mountain Homes was very easy to deal with in that respect."

Green Mountain designs blend traditional decorative details with modern fuctional elements. Homes range from small, do-it-yourself projects to large, substantial family homes. Green Moun-

A Saltbox 34 design offers a garage, an airlock entry and a wood shed.

tain also manufactures kits for town-houses and multifamily structures.

Designs fall into one of four categories, based on size, profile, and roof type. The first category, saltbox homes, comes in 28-foot widths, with houses ranging in length from 30 to 38 feet. Combining historical appeal with maximum solar efficiency, the design's traditional long, sloping roof usually faces north, while the taller façade, primarily of glass, faces south.

The second category consists of gambrel-roof houses and Green Mountain's Model "S" houses. The company bases the designs for its 24-foot-wide gambrel homes on the sturdy, rugged, energy-efficient barns of New England and the Pennsylvania Dutch farm country. These attractive and spacious homes employ such energy-conserving tactics as airlock entrances, strategically placed patio doors and windows, and wood or coal backup heating systems. Model "S" homes, available in lengths from 32 feet to 48 feet, offer a 12″ × 12″ roof pitch and east–west alignment for optimum solar exposure.

Targeted particularly for do-it-your-self builders and first-time homebuyers, the Model "N" homes in the third category are designed to allow for expansion. These houses come with complete plans, a photo-illustrated construction man-ual, and the factory-built kit of parts. "N" models, 16 feet wide, range in length from 18 to 38 feet. They feature a variety of different floor plans and space arrangements, including one design that owners can build in successive phases as their budgets permit.

Colorado model homes, the fourth category, offer single-story living for small families, people living alone, and retirees. Ranging in size from 28′ × 32′ all the way up to 60′ in length, Colorado homes are the only designs that employ conventional stud construction rather than a post and beam frame. Clerestory windows, combined with a low-profile roofline, make these houses unobtrusive on rural sites, but still provide lots of light and air.

In addition to these four house categories, Green Mountain also produces a variety of special designs, including townhouses, recreational structures, commercial buildings, and greenhouse/sunspaces. For those who aren't ready to build a whole new home, sunspaces provide the option of adding a passive

Model N homes are designed for do-it-yourselfers and can easily be expanded.

Gambrel-roof models offer extra headroom on the top story.

solar heating design to an existing house to increase energy efficiency and reduce heating bills.

The Olsens and the Lewises both own saltbox models, while Bill Moody, a New Jersey resident, built a Model "S" home as a ski lodge and vacation home in Grantham, New Hampshire. "We designed the interior ourselves, with three levels—large gathering spaces on the ground floor, with a kitchen and combination living/dining room. Bedrooms are on the second floor, and a large third-level sleeping loft takes care of the guest overflow."

The Olsens designed the interior of their 34-foot saltbox with an eye toward making it their eventual retirement home. "Since both of our mothers are unable to walk well," says Harold, "we put two of the bedrooms downstairs and installed a bath equipped with handicapped facilities. There's one large bedroom upstairs. We liked the flexibility we had to design our own interior. We would send our interior ideas to Jim Kachaturian and he would send us back drawings with changes and explanations. It was pretty easy to get what we wanted. They leave a lot of decisions up to you, so you can come close to your ideal. Since we were first-time builders, in retrospect there are a few things we would do differently—the first time we met with the electrical contractor, he asked us where we wanted the outlet and

An efficient Green Mountain kitchen, designed by the home's owner.

wall switches and we had no idea! Now that we've lived in the house for a while, we do have a few thoughts about what we'd like to change. Nothing major, just a few details."

"It was like building a stick-built house, in terms of getting what you want and having things built to your own special criteria," adds John Lewis. "I enjoyed the experience of building this house so much I'd like to build another one."

Green Mountain homes, with their post and beam framing, are easy to build. "The most unusual part is the foundation," says John. "You should try to find a contractor who's interested in what he's doing, because it's not an ordinary foundation. It's a little complicated if you

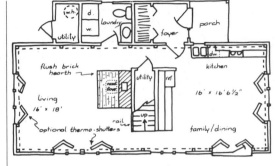

Top: Floorplan for model N38X, designed especially for do-it-yourself builders.

haven't done it before—you have to pay attention."

The Olsens concur. "A lot of contractors don't want to have to deal with anything weird," says Harold. "They pooh-pooh the notion and try to talk you into an ordinary raised ranch. We had to talk to a few contractors before we found one who was willing to take it on. But

Saltbox models offer traditional New England styling along with solar efficiency.

once construction started, we had no problems."

Green Mountain Homes offers lots of construction advice. Jim Kachaturian, or one of his assistants, is always available for consultation and help for people who run into problems. "Once you've decided

"I was nervous about a solar house because I didn't want too many gimmicks—no pipes on the roof or anything like that. But this house is great."

what you want your house to be like," says Harold, "it's really very easy. Green Mountain will give you a quote on the components package for the final design, and under their *refundable* deposit system, you get your money back if you decide not to build. They send you three sets of plans and an illustrated building manual. You can use this material to get quotes from builders and subcontractors. Then you can order your kit and fix up the details with Green Mountain."

The cost of a home kit from Green Mountain ranges from $12,000 for a 695-square-foot Model "N" home that you can build yourself, to $34,000 for an 1,895-square-foot saltbox model which includes a garage. Double these prices to arrive at an estimated finish cost for an owner-built or contracted home, and

add 10–15% more if you intend to hire a contractor to build your house. If, for example, a contractor were to erect and finish the shells of the two homes mentioned above, the total cost would come to $30,000 for the smaller and $97,000 for the larger home. ∎

A Green Mountain saltbox turns its face to the sun.

A Green Mountain Home kit includes the following:

- □ **Container and ducts, with plans for Solar Slab heat mass and exchanger**
- □ **Post and beam wall and roof framing system**
- □ **Outside siding**
- □ **Rigid foam board for outer insulation**
- □ **Plywood sheathing**
- □ **Fiberglass inner insulation and studding**
- □ **Vapor barrier**
- □ **Complete construction plans and illustrated construction manual**
- □ **High-quality insulated windows and doors**

LINDAL CEDAR HOMES

This design from Lindal Cedar Homes features a prow-front, a steeply pitched roof and plenty of windows.

L indal Cedar Homes, based in Seattle, Washington, is the largest manufacturer of cedar homes in the world. Because the company owns and operates its own sawmill and has manufacturing facilities in Seattle and Vancouver, British Columbia, it can better control the quality of the lumber used in its kits. Lindal sells its homes through a network of 125 dealers in the USA and Canada.

Western red cedar, Lindal's primary building material, contains its own natural preservative oils, which protect it against insect infestation, mildew, and rot. Cedar is less prone to warping than most other woods and, because the many spaces between its fibers allow cedar to trap air, it's also a natural insulator. All of these features make cedar one of the finest building materials known, not to mention that it smells good as well. Lindal kiln-dries all of its lumber beforehand to make certain

FRONT ELEVATION

REAR ELEVATION

Sited to face southward, this house becomes an effective solar home.

that it won't twist or warp once the house is constructed. Kiln-drying also makes the wood lighter, which reduces shipping costs. "I chose Lindal because of the high-quality materials and components available, such as Pella-brand windows," says Jean Fiorot, who owns a Lindal home in Croton, New York.

Lindal specializes in heavily insulated houses, including a Polar series of houses for particularly cold climates. "I felt that Lindal offered the best insulated houses on the market, which was important to me," Jean remarks. "I think a lot of builders tend to really skimp on the insulation."

To meet the demands of different climates, Lindal offers various degrees of insulation for the walls, roofs, and floors of its homes. Lindal recommends its standard roof for most climates. Since warm air tends to rise, houses need more insulation in the roof than anywhere else. The standard roof consists of 2×12 rafters filled with 9-inch-thick batts of fiberglass insulation, sealed with a vapor barrier and topped with half-inch plywood sheathing. Drywall or cedar paneling forms the inside ceiling, while shingles or shakes cover the exterior. The standard roof has an R-value of 33.

For harsher climates, Lindal developed the Polar Cap roof. Since 2×12 rafters are the deepest solid rafters available, Lindal developed an open web rafter that can expand from 16 to 24 inches to accommodate more and deeper layers of insulation. The Polar Cap I roof, recommended for warm, humid climates where summer cooling is a top priority, features 9 inches of insulation. The generous air space resulting from the open web design prevents heavy condensation

from forming and damaging the insulation—a common problem in such climates. This roof also has an R-value of 33.

The Polar Cap II roof, for colder climates, employs one layer of 9-inch insulation and a second layer of 3½-inch insulation, for an R-value of 41. The massive Polar Cap III roof, intended for use in arctic climates like Alaska, where the weather reaches extremes of cold,

Top: A typical Lindal interior offers a look at the exposed frame.

Bottom: The massive Polar Cap roof works well with up-to-date designs.

has a 24-inch-deep cavity that can hold up to 18 inches of insulation, for an R-value of 63.

Lindal also offers two different levels of wall insulation. The 7½-inch-thick standard wall features tongue and groove cedar exterior siding applied over Du Pont Tyvek housewrap and ½-inch-thick plywood, with two layers of insulation. One layer overlaps the framing itself, providing a seamless envelope of insulation all the way around the perimeter of the house. Inside the wall, a vapor barrier of heavy polyethylene sheeting seals a second layer. The standard wall has an R-value of 21, while the optional 9-inch-thick Lindal Polar wall offers an R-rating of 29.

Lindal also supplies two different versions of floor insulation. The standard version of the floor employs 2 × 10 floor beams and 2 × 6 joists, with ¾-inch underlayment grade tongue and groove plywood nailed and glued over the joists. Under this goes a layer of reflective foil insulation, which gives the floor an R-value of 12. For colder climates, es-

pecially when building over a crawl space, Lindal recommends the optional Polar floor, with 6 inches of insulation between the floor joists to raise the R-value to 21.

Lindal pays particular attention to insulation around windows and doors. The company offers insulated-core steel doors with an R-value of 14. Its cedar-framed windows have earned a Class A Improved rating: they allow absolutely no air and water infiltration under testing conditions of the utmost severity. All Lindal windows, of whatever style, have cedar instead of aluminum frames, because cedar insulates more effectively. Lindal also fits its windows with a con-

tinuous gasket to cut down on air infiltration and reduce drafts. The double-glazed panes themselves are highly energy efficient. Lindal also offers Heat Mirror glass, which consists of double-glazed glass with a layer of specially treated, heat-reflective polyester film sealed between the panes. In the winter, the reflective coating lets the sunlight in but keeps radiant heat from escaping. In the summer, it acts to block heat from entering the house.

"I used heavy-duty Polar insulated walls, floors, and roof in my home," says Jean. "Along with the super insulation, I employed passive solar techniques. All my windows face to the south and west, with very little glazing on the north wall. I have a freestanding fireplace/wood-stove in the living room, with an uninsulated flue going up to the cathedral ceiling. It's the only source of heat in the house besides the baseboard radiators, which I don't use very often. I find that I use about five hundred gallons of oil a year for heat and hot water in a twenty-four-hundred-square-foot home, which is really pretty low. I believe that

The Gambrel series offers extra headroom on the top floor and a well-insulated roof.

the excellent insulation Lindal supplies is the key to energy conservation. Good insulation—the *best* insulation—was more important to me really than just passive solar features like a sun room or a solar mass or a Trombe wall. I'm also fortunate in that I have a perfect solar site. Lindal gave me a lot of advice on

---

"The excellent insulation Lindal supplies is the key to energy conservation," according to one Lindal homeowner.

---

how to situate my house, and I feel that it has worked out really well."

Lindal offers many standard house designs, all based on a post and beam frame. The framing supports the walls and roof, so that the non-loadbearing interior walls can be placed anywhere. The company distinguishes its three basic design categories by their rooflines—Chalet homes, with steep-pitched roofs and high cathedral ceilings; Gambrels, with double-pitch roofs that wrap down around the second story to create more headroom; and Contemporary houses, with broader roofs, vaulted ceilings, and exposed ceiling beams. The flexibility afforded by the post and beam architecture makes it easy to mix and match rooflines and floorplans from the three categories.

Within each category, Lindal offers different series of house designs that share

the same general characteristics and some similar features. Each series includes a variety of models with different floorplans.

The Chalet category features models with what Lindal calls "prows"—double-angled façades filled with windows that afford sweeping two-story, two-sided views. These houses often feature cathedral ceilings, open beams, and second-story loft spaces. Many prow houses increase the available living space by adding single-story wings. Others include two-story wings, which provide extra floor space in an economical way. Smaller versions have no wings at all, although they can accommodate any desired additions after construction. Chalets are also available in models without the prow front.

Houses in the Gambrel category have distinctive double-pitch roofs that wrap down to form part of the outside walls of the upper story. The higher R-value of the massive roof makes gambrels remarkably energy-efficient. Most Gambrel homes offer two full floors of living space, and some have additional one-story wings. Other models turn the

Opposite page: This prow-front home from the Chalet Series offers lots of glass up front.

Lindal's dramatic designs can accommodate active family lifestyles.

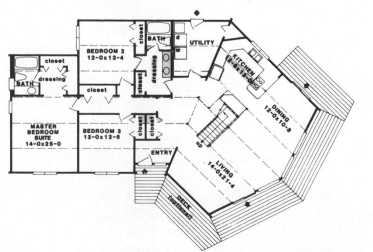

59

A custom design from Lindal supplies 2,439 square feet of elegant comfort.

second story into an open loft and create a cathedral ceiling with exposed beams in the living area, which also includes two-story windows.

The Contemporary category includes a variety of houses: tri-level models that divide the ground floor into two levels separated by a few steps and include a third level on the upper story; homes with T- or L-shaped plans; and split-levels. The Panorama series offers a front wall of floor-to-ceiling glass and can incorporate a prow front. And Lindal designed the Hillside series specifically to make effective use of sloping sites.

In addition to the broad range of stock house plans available, Lindal offers a custom design service. The company's designers can modify its standard floor plans in almost any way desired, whether it involves changing the location of a door or window, enlarging the kitchen, adding an extra bedroom, or almost anything else. Changes are easy to make, and Lindal charges only a small fee for the service, in addition to the cost of any extra materials that the modifications make necessary. Alternatively, Lindal can design a completely new house not based on any of its standard models.

The company calculates its fee for original plans on the square footage of the custom-designed home.

"I appreciated Lindal's design service," says Jean. "I contracted the house myself, and while I'm experienced in construction, I don't know anything about contracting. I felt more comfortable going with a tried-and-true design, because I've heard so many horror stories about dealing with an architect. By buying from Lindal, I was able to beat the architect problem and still have a custom house. I also felt that I could trust the Lindal designers to tell me what was and wasn't feasible, and save me from the possible nightmares of building from scratch.

"Another aspect of the Lindal system that I really appreciated and found helpful was the dealer network," she adds. "I felt very comfortable with my dealer—I knew that he would take an active part in solving problems and was a person I could talk to. I did a lot of work and put in a lot of time, but I really enjoyed the experience."

Prices for Lindal's quality homes range from $20,803 for a 740-square-foot Vegas model from the Chalet Prow se-

Opposite page: Cedar paneling and soaring cathedral ceilings are just two of the exciting interior options Lindal offers.

ries—which features a steep-pitch roof, a glassed-in prow front, and a second-story loft; to $92,326 for a 3,658-square-foot Scarsdale model from the Contemporary executive series—with a broad, low-pitch roof and a full-height second story.

"I thought that my Lindal home was worth what I paid for it," says Jean. "The Lindal was miles above anything else I saw offered as a stickbuilt house. Those were just Sheetrock palaces. The Lindal is really solid." ∎

A typical Lindal package includes:

- The post and beam floor system with twin 2 × 10 floor beams and 2 × 6 floor joists, with ¾″ underlay grade T&G plywood, with glue
- Supporting posts of sturdy 4 × 4 or larger fir
- Exterior walls of kiln-dried, tongue and groove Western red cedar in 1″ or 2″ thickness
- Wall insulation
- Interior partitions of conventional frame 2 × 4 studding covered with drywall, or optional pine or cedar paneling
- Cedar-framed, insulated windows
- Cedar paneling for roof overhangs
- Horizontal glue-laminated roof and loft beams
- Roof system of 2 × 12 rafters, with 9″ fiberglass insulation and ½″ plywood, with interior ceiling liner of drywall or cedar or pine paneling
- Roof covering of browntone fiberglass shingles or handsplit cedar shakes
- Hardware, including locks, nails, caulking, metal connectors, and ridge vents

Package prices do not include the cost of labor, foundation materials, plumbing, heating and electrical systems, cabinetry, or finishing costs.

NORTHERN ENERGY HOMES

Northern Energy Homes specializes in highly energy-efficient homes that combine the strength of post and beam framing with the thermal benefits of R-38 exterior panels. The company manufactures houses in over 250 standard designs, in both contemporary and traditional styles. Almost all of Northern Energy's customers, however, make use of the company's custom design service to adapt one of the standard plans to their specific needs.

Its comprehensive approach to energy-efficient construction allows Northern Energy to produce virtually energy-independent houses — homes that do not require furnaces, electric baseboards, woodburning stoves, or solar heating systems. The exterior panels of a Northern Energy house consist of 8-inch-thick polystyrene insulation sandwiched between an interior surface of pine or Sheetrock and an exterior sub-panel covered with siding selected by the customer. Because windows and doors are foam-sealed directly into the panels during manufacturing, infiltration problems are almost entirely eliminated. Special window treatments and joining techniques for corners and eaves complement the energy benefits of the uninterrupted insulation in the panels.

A superinsulated post and beam house is practical, dependable, and tough.

A ground water heat pump provides each Northern Energy house with heat, hot water, and cooling, while a fresh air exchanger replaces stale air with fresh air from outdoors, recovering in the pro-

Top & bottom: Northern Energy Homes provide energy efficiency without compromising comfort.

cess much of the heat normally lost during ventilation. Northern Energy's combination of energy-saving features results in homes that typically require a quarter of the electricity needed to heat conventional homes, yet maintain a constant temperature year-round.

Because Northern Energy feels confident that its houses offer greater energy advantages than even other super-insulated homes, it offers customers an Energy Consumption Guarantee. For customers who agree to participate in the program, the company guarantees the cost of heat and hot water for two winter seasons. Engineers work with Northern Energy customers to determine projected energy use for their house. If consumption exceeds the targeted figure by more than 25% for each of the two winter seasons covered, the company will reimburse the customer for excess energy expenses. If, on the other hand, a customer's usage falls below the projected amount, Northern Energy will pay them a bonus of $100.

Made up of 8×12 carrying beams, Northern Energy post and beam framing resists stresses and twisting. Pre-cut and notched, the frame is easy to construct. It offers all the versatility and strength typical of post and beam construction, and can play a role in the house's interior decor if left exposed along with the wood panels. Customers can also buy, if they prefer, a conventionally framed house from Northern Energy.

Because each Northern Energy house is designed individually, the company does not have a standard price list, but its houses generally cost $25 to $35 per square foot, the least expensive model being priced at about $35,000. ∎

The following standard materials come with each Northern Energy package:

- Floor and roof framing
- Wall framing, with 1″ tongue and groove knotty pine wall and roof paneling or ½″ waterproof paneling (for post and beam houses); or pre-manufactured polystyrene laminated wall panels (for frame houses)
- 2″ tongue and groove spruce flooring or ¾″ tongue and groove smooth subfloor
- ⁷⁄₁₆″ exterior wall and roof sheathing (exterior glue)
- 8″ expanded polystyrene wall and roof insulation
- Exterior fascia, soffits, and trim materials
- Caulk, nails, hardware, and fasteners
- 235-lb. seal-down roof shingles, ½″ asphalt-impregnated roof cover layment, and 15 lb. felt roofing paper
- Polystyrene foundation wall insulation and 1,600-square-foot 4-mil poly sheet
- Tyvek housewrap
- Exterior siding: redwood clapboard, white cedar, verticle shiplap pine, or clear rough cedar clapboard
- Super-insulated windows
- Insul-core primed exterior doors
- Fresh air heat exchanger
- Ground water heat pump

PACIFIC FRONTIER HOMES

A single-story design from Pacific Frontier nestles comfortably on a wooded site.

Pacific Frontier Homes, based in the redwood logging country of Northern California, manufactures and sells the only packaged redwood homes available. Among commercially marketed wood, redwood has the best specs: the highest insulation value, the lowest flame-spread rating, and the greatest resistance to shrinking and warping—better even than cedar. This combination of qualities makes it easy to care for the exterior. The wood doesn't have to be painted or treated with preservatives. Redwood paneling throughout the interior supplies a mellow, natural beauty, and it can be combined with other interior finishes—such as drywall—for a diversity of effects.

"These are fantastic, very strong houses," says Chris Weiss of Albuquerque, New Mexico, who built a redwood addition to his own home using materials supplied by Pacific Frontier, and another Pacific Frontier package specifically for resale. "Redwood is naturally resistant to rot, mildew, and insect infestation. That's why those trees last so long and grow so tall."

Pacific Frontier offers a complete redwood post and beam home that features an

extremely sturdy and relatively easy-to-build framing system of solid redwood beams. The blend of barnlike construction methods and redwood timbers results in an easily maintained home with a casual feeling to it. "I've always been an admirer of post and beam construction," says Chris. "This house is simple to put together—you only need a hammer, a saw, and a tape measure. In addition, the construction method results in such a strong house that the insurance premiums are lower."

After the framing crew puts up and braces the pre-cut post and beam frame—including the roof rafters—the horizontal tongue and groove redwood interior paneling is placed over the posts. Roofers lay the tongue and groove pine roof decking onto the rafters, leaving the framing exposed on the interior—which results in a rugged, rustic appearance. The crew then covers the roof and walls with 4×8 sheets of rigid insulation—overlaying it with waterproof paper—and installs the windows and doors. Next, they apply the 8-inch wide vertical redwood tongue and groove exterior siding and roof shakes. After that, the interior finishing can be completed at leisure.

"The frame is very simple to put together, and goes up quickly," says Chris. "You just put the pre-cut frame up, and the rest of the materials can be cut to fit on site, like the paneling. It's really a

breeze. An advantage for the amateur builder is that this is a very forgiving house. It's easy to fix your mistakes. Two people can build this house—in fact, one person could build it. Three people can put it together really fast. The package is geared to people with adventure in their soul and the desire to save money on a superior home."

The Eagle's Nest, featured in issues of *Professional Builder*, *Popular Science*, and *Sunset*, is Pacific Frontier's most popular model. It offers an exciting variety of open-plan interior spaces, cathedral ceilings, and lofts, in combination with outdoor terraces, second-story decks with railed catwalks, window walls for passive solar heating, and clerestory windows tucked away under the eaves to light the upper-level spaces. The innovative use of limited space results in houses that seem extra large because of all their nooks and crannies.

Bill Low built a modified Eagle's Nest in Sebastopol, California, a small town northwest of San Francisco. "I'm an architect by training, so I designed the house myself. I took the basic Eagle's

Pacific Frontier offers many solar designs, with south-facing windows and sky-lit roofs.

A redwood kit under construction.

Nest, and expanded it and improved on it somewhat to meet our needs, so I had just what I wanted. The house is sixteen-hundred square feet, with a passive solar heating system—lots of south-facing windows and a masonry thermal mass under the floor to retain heat. I built it just this year—I started in April and finished in July."

*R*edwood post and beam construction and a combination of rustic and contemporary detailing highlight each Pacific Frontier home.

The smaller of the two standard Eagle's Nest models, typically about 1,200 square feet, includes a downstairs bedroom, an upper-story loft with adjacent deck, lots of skylights, and a tiled sunspace. The larger model offers three bedrooms on two levels: the master bedroom with fireplace and private deck upstairs; a smaller bedroom next door, also with its own deck; and a third bedroom downstairs. This 1,700-square-foot design also includes abundant glass and a tiled sunspace for solar heating.

Pacific Frontier offers a variety of models and floor plans for both single-story and two-story homes in addition to the Eagle's Nest. Redwood post and beam construction and a combination of rustic and streamlined contemporary detailing

highlight all of the models. Some, like the Frontier II series, are low-slung one-story homes with broad roof overhangs, lots of glass, and raised clerestory windows that admit sunlight into the core of the house from above.

The Frontier VI series has more of a saltbox profile, with a higher, two-story façade oriented to the south and a prominent window wall for efficient passive solar heating. The roof slopes gently down and back to a single story in the rear, and large redwood decks extend out on either side of the house, forming a T-shape. A small loft space on the upper level provides extra space, and features a balcony that looks over the cathedral-ceilinged living room.

The Frontier VII model offers twin hipped-roof pavilions, a wraparound deck, and clerestory windows under the eaves. The Frontier VIII has a similar profile: a two-story central square, surrounded on the front and sides by a broad redwood deck, adjoins a single-story wing that runs along the back of the house. The Frontier XI, specifically designed as a passive solar house, offers a

Post and beam frame and redwood wall paneling go up quickly.

The interior of a Pacific Frontier house offers the warmth of redwood.

variety of options—such as Trombe walls, masonry thermal masses, sunspaces or atriums with tiled floors to retain heat, and skylights that admit the sun.

The prices of standard Pacific Frontier models vary according to size. A single-story standard model from the Frontier II series, with 850 square feet consisting of two bedrooms, a combination living/dining room, and a fireplace, costs about $28,099 for the kit. Larger homes, such as the Frontier III Cabrillo—1,658 square feet with three bedrooms, two baths, separate living and dining rooms, a deck, and a porch—cost $44,152. A standard Eagle's Nest kit, at 1,200 square feet, costs $29,940. ■

A typical Pacific Frontier package contains the following materials:

- □ Pre-cut 4-inch air-seasoned redwood posts
- □ Pre-cut 4-inch Douglas fir rafters
- □ 1½ × 6 interior horizontal redwood paneling in random lengths, air-seasoned, tongue and groove, roughsawn on one side
- □ Double foil–faced urethane insulation, 1″ thick for walls, 2″ thick for roof
- □ 15-lb. saturated roofing felt
- □ Exterior siding of 1 × 6 random-length clear kiln-dried tongue and groove redwood, roughsawn on one side

- □ Interior partition walls with redwood posts, in random lengths, and tongue and groove redwood siding
- □ Roof decking of tongue and groove kiln-dried Ponderosa pine
- □ Dual-glazed windows with bronzetone aluminum frames
- □ Insulated Peachtree brand exterior doors, pre-hung
- □ Materials for redwood porch
- □ Redwood exterior trim

Kits from Pacific Frontier Homes do not include subflooring, cabinetry or interior doors, electrical or plumbing material, or nails.

SAWMILL RIVER POST & BEAM

Sawmill River Post & Beam produces its house packages in a traditional water-powered sawmill that was built in 1750. The last of thirteen such mills that operated during the nineteenth century in the Leverett, Massachussets area, the mill remains much the same as it was a hundred years ago. When they bought the mill in 1972, Sawmill River's owners restored the 1889 Leffel turbine, and now the mill's fifty-inch circular blade can cut timbers up to forty feet long.

Sawmill River manufactures true post and beam houses in contemporary, traditional, and country contemporary styles. By using plentiful, readily available native materials, the company keeps costs down and maintains strict control over the quality of its houses. The company engineers its kits for fast, easy construction—workers can complete a weathertight and insulated shell in a matter of days. Its short timber lengths weigh less, so builders can handle them easily, and its special corner bracing and simple lap joints mean the houses can go up without the use of heavy machinery.

Sawmill River supplies its houses in a choice of three kit packages. PAC I packages contain the complete pre-cut frame only, although the price does include design services, drawings, and on-site technical assistance. PAC II kits include everything supplied with PAC I kits, plus exterior siding, windows, custom

Striking window design and a cathedral ceiling accentuate the effect of exposed beams.

glass, second floor decking, and stair and door options. Both of these packages appeal to those who wish to do some of the work on their own home, or who have hired a local builder to do the work for them. PAC III kits supply all materials and labor to complete a fully insulated, weathertight shell on the customer's foundation. Customers need only finish the interior.

Customers can adapt any of Sawmill River's standard designs to their own needs at no extra cost. The company's regular line of homes includes saltboxes, gambrel-roofed houses, capes and colonials. Ranging in size from 1,086 square feet to 1,880 square feet, these houses cost anywhere from $11,760 for a small PAC I kit to $39,700 for 1,644-square-foot PAC III model. The homes can incorporate a number of features, including central chimneys, breezeways, and attached garages.

In addition to its basic line, Sawmill River offers a Classic Cape series designed for easy expansion. The company has designed a whole range of expansion options—family rooms, studies, guest-rooms, breezeways, and garages—especially for each house in the series. Customers can choose from among these options when planning their homes, or build the basic units only. The basic units offer two or three bedrooms and price out at anywhere from $18,800 for a 1,248-square-foot PAC II kit ($37,900 for the PAC III version) to

$50,300 for a 1,664-square foot PAC III kit ($25,000 for the PAC II version). Extension options range in price from $1,350 for a small PAC II breezeway connector to $17,600 for a 440-square-foot PAC III family room.

Sawmill River also offers a Smaller Smarter series of homes designed to make the most of limited space to create efficient, economical homes. These saltboxes and capes supply anywhere from 890 to 1,594 square feet of useable space and come in PAC I, II, or III packages. Prices for Smaller Smarter homes start at $7,000 for the smallest frame-only kit and range up to $47,400 for the largest complete weathertight insulated shell package. ▪

The materials supplied with each Sawmill River house depend on the customer's choice of PAC I, II, or III options. The PAC III complete insulated weathertight shell includes:

- PAC I package: Pre-cut rough sawn timber frame of native eastern white pine, including all posts, plate beams, floor joists, rafters, window framing corner braces, and nailers, plus ash wood pegs, hardened spikes, and steel pin fasteners
- PAC II package: Andersen windows, Peachtree patio doors, fixed glass, pine exterior doors with hardware, pine stair set, 1–½-inch tongue and groove kiln dried white pine second floor decking, and ⅞-inch rough sawn pine shiplap exterior siding
- Foundation cap
- Basement stairs
- Wall and roof insulation (walls R-19, roof R-30)
- Fiberglass-backed asphalt roof shingles
- Skylights
- Galvanized nails, aluminum flashing, and caulking

SHELTER-KIT

A s Henry David Thoreau once wrote, "There is the same fitness in a man's building his own house that there is in a bird's building his own nest." Shelter-Kit, a small kit home manufacturer based in Tilton, New Hampshire, believes that everyone should be able to build their own home. The company manufactures two basic house models — available in three different sizes — designed especially for the build-it-yourselfer.

Andy Prokosch, president of Shelter-Kit, says, "We offer high-quality buildings to people who want to put up their own houses, which are very flexible in terms of what you can do with them. About ninety-nine percent of the people who buy homes from us build them themselves. It works. We've never had anyone quit, we've never had anyone give up. We've been doing it since 1970, so I guess that both the product and the approach work reasonably well."

Unit One, the smaller of the two models available from Shelter-Kit, is a single-story 12' × 12' unit with a shed roof, and costs about $4,500 to build. Shelter-Kit considers the Unit One to be a modular unit, and sells several stock house plans designed around clusters of Unit Ones,

to which it adds smaller 9′ × 12′ units — called enclosed porches — for variety and additional floorspace. These single-story units can be combined in a number of different ways to create a nearly endless range of single-story homes, all different.

Just outside of Hallsville, Missouri, for example, Dave and Debin Benish built a 1,300-square-foot Shelter-Kit home consisting of four Unit One modules and six enclosed porches. "We had never built anything from scratch before, although we'd both had experience doing odd jobs of carpentry," says Debin. "We spent about three years reading and studying about homebuilding before we actually decided to go ahead and do it ourselves. We wanted to buy land and end up with a house that was completely paid for, so that we could quit our jobs and go into business for ourselves without house payments hanging over our heads. Building the house ourselves turned out to be the only way we could afford it."

"Shelter-Kit homes are often bought by people who might not otherwise be able to afford their own home," Andy Prokosch notes. "One of my major interests in starting this company was to provide good, solid housing at a low cost to the consumer. I see Shelter-Kit as a viable house alternative for many different sectors of the population. On the other hand, many people buy Unit Ones as barebones summer retreats, and build them up in the woods without plumbing or electricity."

Many people also build home kits from Shelter-Kit as year-round residences. Lofthouse 20 and Lofthouse 16 are designed specifically for this purpose — Shelter-Kit simply stretched the modular idea to fit a two-story unit. The

larger unit, Lofthouse 20, comes in a standard 20′ × 24′ size, while the Lofthouse 16 is usually 16′ × 16′. Both can be of any length, however, and add-on units of various sizes — called lean-tos, extensions, and porches — are also available.

Alice and Phil Innes of Brattleboro, Vermont, built a Lofthouse 20 with lean-to additions on both sides. "We spent the main portion of our money on a good piece of land, because my wife is a horticulturist," explains Phil. "We didn't have a lot of money left over, and a do-it-yourself kit house provided a welcome solution. Neither of us had ever built so much as a chicken coop before. My wife and I built eighty-five percent of the house, the largest two-story kit Shelter-Kit offers, ourselves. The house was easy to do, really — interior finishing took the longest. Alice did the plumbing with a plumbing kit from Shelter-Kit. They really provided us with a lot of advice,

Top: The rugged post and beam frame is designed to make construction simple for the do-it-yourselfer.

Bottom: Two people can build a Unit One in four days.

and on a few occasions Andy Prokosch came down to lend a hand and the benefit of his advice."

Shelter-Kit takes a number of steps to ensure that building one of its houses is a satisfying experience for the buyer. The Shelter-Kit construction manual, for instance, remarkably clear and easy to read and understand, contains a step-by-step account of the construction process, with hand-drawn illustrations, which amateur builders find easier to read than blueprints.

"It's designed for people who know absolutely nothing about how to build, and contains a glossary of terms and techniques, and a nail size chart," says Andy. "It was a really tedious thing to write, because it's so detailed, and I imagine that if you know anything about building, it's probably very tedious to read. But if people follow it exactly, they'll put the buildings together with no trouble at all. One thing that's important about using our kit is that it comes out right. As you do this, you gain a wonderful sense of accomplishment. You've really done something—you've created this. It's a tremendous feeling. It's very hard to describe: you can't advertise it, you can't sell it, but it's there, and most peo-

ple don't know about it until they're actually into construction."

Shelter-Kit's post and beam construction system gives the amateur builder a number of design options. Because the interior walls are non-load-bearing, buyers have lots of leeway in developing the interior layout. For example, buyers can place sliding glass doors across the full width of the front wall, and other doors and windows in virtually any location.

By using different types of doors, siding, and windows— which Shelter-Kit offers as options—homeowners can dramatically change the exterior appearance of either the Unit One or the Lofthouse. For example, use of clapboard siding, traditional double-hung windows, and hinged doors on a Lofthouse, instead of the sliding doors and windows supplied with the standard kit, makes the unit look just like a traditional Cape Cod home. Shelter-Kit customers can apply different sidings directly over the standard finish at any time after completing the house.

Because Shelter-Kit prices its houses per module, each assemblage of units has a different price. The Unit One catalog features combinations of Unit One

The interior of a Unit One is sunny and surprisingly spacious.

A Lofthouse under construction.

modules in a variety of configurations, from one to four bedrooms, including one large home that consists of nine Unit Ones and seven decks. Prices of Unit Ones in the standard configurations range from $5,085 for a single Unit One with deck to $24,390 for a three-bedroom plan. Prices for special arrangements of Unit Ones, with enclosed porches, decks, and different types of windows and doors can be supplied on request.

A standard 16' × 16' Lofthouse 16 costs $8,545, not including windows or doors. A 20' × 24' Lofthouse 20 costs $13,475. Lean-tos, extensions, porches, and decks can cost anywhere from $390 to $3,170, depending on size. ■

The Lofthouse adapts to a number of different styles.

Here's what's included in a Unit One kit:

- 4 × 4 Douglas fir structural posts
- 2 × 10 spruce floor joists and headers
- 2 × 10 Douglas fir or Southern yellow pine rafters
- 2 × 10 spruce roof joists
- 2 × 4 spruce studs, used as nailing points on siding
- Pine and plywood exterior sheathing for siding, flooring, and roofing
- Weather sealing for roof, frame, and joints
- One set of four-panel sliding glass doors, with bronzetone aluminum frame and tempered glass
- One two-panel sliding window, with bronzetone aluminum frame and insulated glass
- Clerestory window for installation above sliding glass doors
- All hardware necessary to complete construction

Complete site preparation and construction manual porch and deck kits will contain similar materials in smaller quantities. Other sizes and types of windows and doors are available as options. Specifications for Lofthouse kits and Lofthouse extensions include the following:

- 4 × 4 Douglas fir posts and joists
- 3½ × 12 floor trusses of Southern yellow pine
- Spruce floor plates
- Spruce rafters, either 2 × 6 or 2 × 8
- Ridgepole of 2 × 8 or 2 × 10 spruce
- 2 × 4 spruce studs
- First and second floor flooring of ¾ tongue and groove plywood, with exterior glue
- Roofing of ⅝-inch plywood with exterior glue, 230-lb. self-seal 3 tab asphalt shingles
- Exterior siding of ⅝-inch roughsawn texture 1-11 plywood
- Pine corner boards and window/door trim
- All hardware necessary to complete house
- Complete site preparation and construction manual
- Windows and doors as specified

TIMBERPEG

imberpeg originally manufactured and sold a line of small buildings known as Cluster Sheds. Designed for use singly or in groups, these 192- to 512-square-foot units offered an economical option for those in need of weekend retreats, studio/workshops, or simple primary residences. Timberpeg still produces Cluster Sheds, but has expanded its catalog to include a range of gambrels, saltboxes, and capes.

Timberpeg's rugged post and beam frames offer the strength, thermal benefits, and interior planning flexibility of all post and beam structures. Mortise and tenon joints pegged with oak trunnels add extra strength to the frame. An uninterrupted sandwich of insulation wraps the frame, increasing energy efficiency. Rough-sawn 1 × 12 white pine boards finish the exterior walls, while hand-split cedar shakes complete the roof. Customers can finish interior surfaces in pine or wallboard.

The basic Timberpeg line includes contemporary and traditional gambrel and saltbox models as well as a number of standard Cluster Shed combinations.

Top: A timberpeg Barnhouse with optional deck and dormer windows.

Bottom: Interiors feature beamed ceilings—the exposed structure of the house itself.

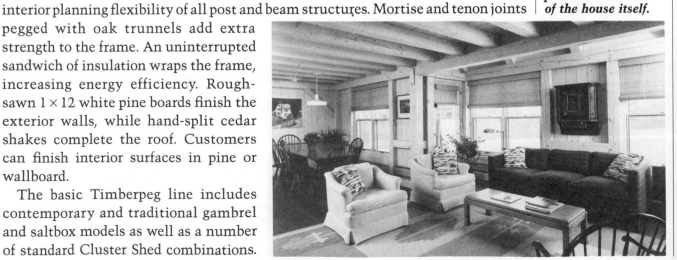

One example, the Timberpeg Design #3638, combines a traditional gambrel with a Cluster Shed. The design adapts the Cluster Shed to serve as a wing that connects the main house with a two-car garage. This wing contains a spacious family room, while the main structure includes three bedrooms, three baths, a living/dining area, and a kitchen with a breakfast nook.

Timberpeg offers a standard line of variations on its basic Barnhouse design, a 1,236-square-foot house designed for comfortable living in less space. The variations include houses offering up to 3,584 square feet of living space. Customers can adapt the largest model—a traditional cape—to meet their design needs in a number of ways. The standard floorplan includes a two-car garage attached to the house by a porch, a family room, library, and parlor, a large kitchen, a dining room opening onto a second porch, four bedrooms, three baths, and two half-baths.

The Temperate Series, featuring shallow roof pitches with broad overhangs, provides customers building in warmer climates with a number of advantages. The overhangs protect the houses from both rain and sunlight, while insulation in the walls, roofs, and windows help keep interiors cool. The three houses in this series have a contemporary look and run 1,520 to 2,272 square feet in size.

For those in cooler climates, Timberpeg markets a line of solar homes. The five houses in the Solar Series make use of passive solar heating techniques to maximize energy efficiency. One model adds active solar collectors for further solar benefits. Each solar house includes a woodburning stove and incorpo-

Timberpeg Design 3638 combines a traditional Gambrel with a Cluster Shed wing and an attached garage.

rates features such as minimized exterior wall area, generous south-facing glass, triple glazing on north, east, and west faces, exposed interior masonry, open-plan interiors, air-lock entries, and extra insulation in exterior walls and roofs.

Prices for Timberpeg kits start at $7,273 for the 192-square-foot Cluster Shed #1, which customers can complete for $16,000 to $21,000. The most expensive Timberpeg model—the 3,584-square-foot traditional cape described above—runs $90,160 for the kit and costs anywhere from $195,000 to $225,000 to complete. ■

Timberpeg packages include the following:

- ☐ **Floor system, main and upper levels**
- ☐ **Pre-cut timber framing**
- ☐ **Interior and exterior wall system and insulation**
- ☐ **Roof system with insulation**
- ☐ **Andersen Permashield windows**
- ☐ **Exterior doors**
- ☐ **Sliding glass doors**
- ☐ **Roof windows**
- ☐ **Hardware**

The solar series replaces some of the windows with high-performance glass, and adds extra insulation.

YANKEE BARN HOMES

Ellen and Nancy Weinert own a Yankee Barn home in Grantham, New Hampshire. "We moved in about a year and a half ago," says Nancy. "We've been here two winters. It's really a wonderful house. We planned it as our eventual retirement home, but right now it's great for vacation trips and ski weekends. Our grandchildren really love it."

Allen agrees. "We chose a Yankee Barn home because we liked the appearance of it. While we were deciding on what kind of home to build, we went around and looked at lots of houses, and talked to builders about how much it would cost, and we decided on Yankee Barn. We saw another one of these houses that we liked, and found out who made it, and decided we wanted one like it. We really liked the beams, and the whole general ambience of the house. It's easy to get what you want with Yankee Barn Homes."

Yankee Barn Homes, based in Grantham, manufactures post and beam kit homes that feature antique timbers reclaimed from historic New England structures like manufacturing mills. The resawn timbers create a unique ambience inside the houses, imparting an air of tradition and warmth to even the newest home. The combination of exposed antique timbers and careful detailing—such as nails with hand-wrought heads—produces an attractive blend of contemporary design and solid, old-fashioned comfort.

Yankee Barn entered the kit home

business in 1968. The original model, and still the most popular, is the Mark I Yankee Barn Home. This house features barn-like styling derived from the design of historic New England farmhouses. Comfortable, intimate interiors highlight the standard Mark I — 25 feet wide and 45 feet long with 7-foot-high ceilings. Yankee Barn chairman Emil Hanslin owns a Mark I that features a two-story, cathedral-ceilinged living room — an element which, he acknowledges, "has become something of a Yankee Barn trademark."

The Mark I adapts to all kinds of interior and exterior variations, both major and minor. Owners can customize their homes in many ways, whether by adding a single-story shed to create a saltbox rather than a barn profile or by using clapboards instead of vertical siding for a more traditional look. And Yankee Barn makes it easy for customers to make its standard house larger or smaller. All Yankee Barn homes employ an 8-foot module, so increasing or decreasing the length by that amount — or multiples of it — is quite simple. Alternatively, Yankee Barn offers a number of optional one-story additions — such as granaries (long slope-roof sheds that run the length of the house), greenhouses (sunroom spaces), and foyers — which can increase the width or change the profile of the basic rectangular house when used. In addition, each Yankee Barn model can accommodate a single-story ell addition.

The Prairie Barn model, based on a Midwestern barn prototype, represents Yankee Barn's top of the line — the largest and most luxurious home it offers. Like their Midwestern ancestors, these designs feature roof overhangs and roof

prows that serve a practical as well as an aesthetic function: they shade the interior from the sun's heat and protect the house against the elements.

A standard Prairie Barn is 26 feet wide, but optional additions, as described above, can increase the width by 9 feet. The standard length, which can be increased or decreased in 8-foot increments, is 48 feet. Eight-foot-high ceil-

Top and bottom: Exposed beams and soaring cathedral ceilings distinguish the interior of a home from Yankee Barn.

ings make for a cozy interior, and an ell addition (14′×29′) can add even more space. The Prairie Barn plan allows for a lot of "custom" standard options, including hot tub rooms and cathedral ceilings in the living room. Yankee Barn is so proud of this model that it has designed a portfolio of special adaptations solely for the Prairie Barn.

Yankee Barn Carriage Houses feature a unique type of construction, in which the roof trusses rather than the walls bear the weight of the roof, as in a post and beam home. Thus, the center line of posts is not necessary and the interior of the house remains completely clear. Like the Prairie Barn and the Mark I, this house type represents another adaptation of a nineteenth-century architectural form—in this case, an urban carriage house. With dimensions of 24′×32′, which can also be increased in 8-foot increments, the Carriage House makes a good home for a small family. Additions of a granary or foyer can increase the width by eight feet as well. The 7½-foot ceilings create an intimate air, while a 16′×24′ ell can add more space if desired. This type of construction requires fewer supporting posts than other Yankee Barn designs, making Carriage Houses ideally suited

A rugged Prairie Barn exterior.

to the use of spectacular expanses of exterior glass—a real advantage for sites with a view.

Smaller than other Yankee Barn models, Studio Barns make good retirement or vacation homes. This design series offers several different basic designs, lots of options, and the added appeal of energy efficiency and low maintenance. Because of the post and beam structure, the walls bear the weight of the roof, and the customer can plan interiors with a great deal of freedom.

"One of the things we like about Yankee Barn is the fact that you can do so many things with the basic design," says Nancy Weinert, who owns a Studio Barn with her husband Allen. "We changed this house around so much from the way it was originally, you wouldn't believe it. You can make a lot of changes with these post and beam houses because the interior is open—there are no supporting walls inside the house. There are some limitations, but on the whole you can pretty much do what you want. We added a whole entry hall, and changed

Opposite page: Wood paneling helps to create an informal ambience.

Bottom: A diagram reveals the post and beam structure of a typical Yankee Barn home.

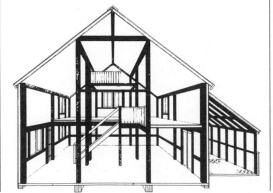

the bedroom completely. With the eight-by-eight modules, it's easy to extend the building or make it wider. The addition is identical—indistinguishable from the main body of the house. We added an extra eight feet for an entry hall, because in the original plan, you entered right into the living room. We didn't like that, so we just added eight feet, putting some of it into making the living room a little bit larger, and the rest of it into a hall."

The Weinerts changed some other details of their home, too. "We changed the woodstove into a fireplace," says Nancy. "We took out the closet that was in the plan, and had the builder add on another one. We made the master bedroom and bath into one big room, with a jacuzzi.

We put a cathedral ceiling in the bedroom, with a skylight over the tub. The builder said he'd never worked on a project that had so many changes. We'd come up every weekend and say, 'No, we've changed our minds, we want such and such!'"

All Yankee Barn houses, whatever their style or size, incorporate the same fine structural materials. Customers can choose a frame either of resawn antique timbers or new Douglas fir. The wall materials wrap around the outside of the post and beam frame, creating a seamless envelope of insulation, which makes Yankee Barn houses highly energy-efficient. To add to this inherent efficiency, Yankee Barn insulates the walls of its

Many choices of add-on units and window placement make every Yankee Barn home a custom design.

homes using rigid foam insulation with a high R-value, and includes a Du Pont Tyvek air/moisture infiltration barrier. Made of spun polyolefin fiber, the barrier prevents heat from escaping and moisture from entering. The insulation board and moisture barrier are sandwiched between Eastern pine exterior siding and plywood sheathing.

On the inside, wall surfaces can be paneled in wood or finished with gypsum wallboard. Yankee Barn supplies many different choices of interior trim for windows, doors, and walls: from rustic antique roughsawn timber to smooth-finished fir. The trim can match or contrast with the exposed structural frame. And choice of trim extends to the posts and headers surrounding interior doors, closets, and partitions, as well as to the skylight support beams, which are not part of the structural shell. Wrought-head nails, which come with the standard package, add a traditional note.

Yankee Barn supplies thermal barrier

T he resawn antique timbers impart an air of tradition and warmth to even the newest home.

---

dual-glazed aluminum sliding windows with half-screens. Those who want a more traditional look can purchase aluminum-clad wood casement windows or wood double-hung windows with grids for a slightly higher price. The pine exte-

rior doors arrive pre-hung for on-site installation.

Yankee Barn builds its four-foot-wide stressed-skin roof panels in the factory, and ships them along with the rest of the kit. This method makes it fast and easy to attach the roof after raising the rest of the frame. The panels contain three and a quarter inches of rigid foam insulation, with an R-value of 26. After installing the roof panels, the owner or contractor can finish them with roofing supplies bought locally, using anything from cedar shakes to standing seam metal roofing, depending on the climate.

Yankee Barn furnishes foundation blueprints so that the house can be built with either a full basement or a slab foundation. The company manufactures

Self-supporting post and beam framing permits the use of lots of glass.

its own laminated yellow pine decking, available in random lengths and widths, to cover the first-floor ceiling beams and form the second floor, creating country-style floors above and pine ceilings below. The company also manufactures floor panels similar to those it makes for the roof. Customers can install these instead of decking and cover them with finish flooring of their own choice. They can use anything from carpeting to linoleum, including yellow pine plank floors — available from Yankee Barn — which are similar to the decking but only available in uniform widths. The sound-insulating qualities of the panels provide an added benefit for those concerned about potential noise problems. Both the decking and the panels rest directly on the timbers when installed. Because the flooring system doesn't employ conventional floor joists, the ceiling beams — like the wall supports — remain exposed to view. This results in more headroom — so tall people aren't always knocking their heads — and adds to the rustic ambience of the interior.

Yankee Barn also manufactures specialty millwork items for use in its houses. These high-quality details include interior doors of white pine, with optional thumblatches, decorative straps, and hinges that complement the carefully established rustic atmosphere. Closet doors receive the same attention — Yankee Barn customers can choose pine or simulated barn board, either with the appropriate rustic hardware. Stairs and loft ladders, constructed from antique timbers, are assembled on site, as are balcony rails, posts, and balusters.

Depending on the size of the house,

construction of the shell usually takes about ten days, if completed by a crew of four working under the guidance of an experienced supervisor recommended by Yankee Barn.

The Weinerts are very happy with their house. "It's easy to heat," says Nancy. "Sometimes it's *too* hot. We're thinking of putting in blinds for the skylights, once we move up here to live full time. We have a woodstove in the basement and additional baseboard heating for really cold days, as well as the fireplace. But with the fireplace in use, we

All staircases are custom-designed in the factory, and then built on site.

don't turn the heat on, even in winter."

According to Yankee Barn's price list, the cost of a Studio Barn Cape like the Weinerts' (without figuring in the cost of the numerous changes they made during construction) comes to between $82,634 and $91,816. These prices include everything but sitework and foundation costs, including the cost of a general contrac-

tor. As a general rule, owners can save 10-15% on the total cost by acting as their own general contractor, depending on the section of the country in which they build. ■

Above: Exterior sliding shutters give a Studio Barn a snappy look.

Here's what comes in a standard Yankee Barn package:

- Post and beam frame of either resawn antique timbers or new timbers of Douglas fir
- Exterior walls of Eastern pine siding, spun olefin moisture barrier, rigid foam insulation, and plywood sheathing
- Interior walls of paneling or wallboard
- Thermal-barrier, dual-glazed aluminum sliding windows, standard. Other types of windows available as options.
- Pre-hung pine exterior doors and aluminum-frame sliding doors
- Roof system of 4'-wide stressed-skin panels to be assembled on site
- All interior trim
- Decking for upper floors
- All miscellaneous materials required for assembly of kit
- All construction drawings and prints, along with a construction guide

Left: Three examples of the many different interior finishing choices available from Yankee Barn Homes.

PANELIZED AND MODULAR HOMES

*P*anelized and modular homes arrive at a building site more completely pre-assembled than all other types of kit homes, so they require the least amount of on-site labor. At the factory, workers have cut all the lumber, laid much of the electrical wiring, and even installed doors and windows. Manufacturers of these homes promote factory construction, with its automated processes, as more precise than on-site construction. Companies employ many quality control inspectors to examine each house component before it ever reaches the building site.

The amount of finishing work remaining after the manufacturer's crew leaves the site distinguishes panelized from modular houses. For a panelized home, the company ships factory-built wall panels to the site, and a construction crew — usually with the help of a crane — erects them on the foundation to form a finished shell. The panels usually come with exterior sheathing, insulation, drywall, and electrical outlets already installed. Depending on the package, the crew may also put in interior partitions.

A modular house, by contrast, leaves the factory 90 to 95 percent complete. Even the rugs, wallpaper, and appliances arrive in place. Modular home options often include bathrooms and kitchens, completely installed down to the wiring and plumbing. Motorists may see these houses, in two sections, moving slowly down interstate highways on the backs of flatbed trucks. Crews join the sections, or modules, into a single structure at the site.

Construction crews can erect both panelized and modular buildings quickly. They can usually put the walls, floors, and roof of a panelized house in place and ready the structure for interior finishing in no more than a day to a day-and-a-half. They can put together modular homes, which arrive

with more finished interiors, even faster.

Modular homes come in a large selection of styles and sizes. They also present the novice builder with the least complicated and most finished construction option; the manufacturer's crew puts the house in place on the foundation, virtually eliminating subcontracting and do-it-yourself tasks with most designs. For those needing a completely finished home they can occupy quickly, the modulars remain the first building option to consider.

Panelized kits come in a huge range of styles, including contemporary, traditional, solar, and even geodesic domes. Manufacturers can use the panel method to form the walls, floors, and roofs for just about any type of house except for log homes.

The design flexibility of panelized homes enables manufacturers to maintain architectural and engineering staffs to help customers achieve their dreams. In effect, hiring a panelized house manufacturer resembles hiring an architect—but without the high fees. The design can originate in a sketch, a plan book, or a magazine article. Customers can get *exactly* what they want, from a tiny vacation hideaway to a Victorian mansion.

Both types of houses require more advance planning than do pre-cut post and beam or log homes. The customer must make many final decisions before the factory work can start. During the construction of a log home, for example, builders can move a bathroom or shift a window, but they would find it difficult to make similar changes in a modular or panelized house. ■

ACORN STRUCTURES

A few years ago, in the late 1970s, Mary Catherwood of Stamford, Connecticut, became interested in building an energy-efficient home. "I already owned a house, an adorable little nineteenth-century cottage, but the heating bills were enormous. I owned some property just down the road from where I was living, and I thought, Why not build a house? The tax benefits were great, and I was especially interested in the energy tax credit [no longer available—ed.]. I became interested in Acorn because the company received consistently favorable mention whenever I came across it in my research." In 1982, she decided to build an Acorn Independence Series house. "I had written down a list of things I wanted in my house, and figured out what kind of house would accommodate everything I already owned—and Acorn really seemed to fit the bill."

Acorn Structures, a leading manufacturer of panelized homes, has been making kit houses for almost forty years. Originally established as a producer of single-family homes that helped relieve the acute post–World War II housing shortage, Acorn later went on to produce other manufactured structures as well,

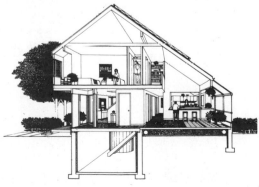

Above: The Country House 3500 offers 5,844 square feet of living space on three levels.

Opposite page: Top & bottom: Open-plan interiors highlight the generous use of natural wood.

Left: Homes by Acorn often feature a saltbox profile.

including commercial and multifamily dwellings.

Acorn's panelized houses, based on a four-foot module, combine design flexibility with energy efficiency. Specializing in passive and active solar models, Acorn offers over fifty standard home designs from which customers can pick and choose, and features a custom design service that buyers can use to customize Acorn's standard plans or to create their own original homes.

Acorn maintains a permanent staff of designers and architects to work with customers at no extra charge. Alternatively, customers can hire their own architects, and Acorn will design a house package following the architects' plans. Such a package would include a full set of working drawings and all the house components. Access to Acorn's design staff helps ensure that buyers end up with homes that best fit their needs, as Mary discovered: "I ran into a problem — the percolation test on the soil showed that my lot had a groundwater problem, so I couldn't dig a basement. The house had to be redesigned for a slab foundation. Acorn did the redesign without charge.

"All things considered," she continues, "designing the house was fun. I loved going up to Acton, Massachusetts, and sitting down at a table with an architect and a big roll of paper. I knew pretty much what I wanted, and that was a big help."

Acorn designs range from traditional Cape Cod models (the Suncape series) to larger country home designs (the Cottage and Country Home series, reminiscent of turn-of-the-century Shingle-style homes), to contemporary designs with dramatic steep-pitch roofs, window-walls, and open-plan interiors incorporating cathedral ceilings and overhanging second-story lofts and balconies. Other design series include simpler models designed especially for small families, first-time homeowners, and retirees.

Mary describes her house as "kind of a contemporary Cape. The south wall is all glass, and I have a sunroom that also provides a source of heat by collecting the sun's warmth in the tile floor. From there it circulates into the rest of the house. Acorn calls it an 'isolated gain sunspace.' I designed it so that a screened breezeway opens off of the sunroom, and so does my bedroom—it keeps it really toasty! Then sliding doors lead to the living room. I love the indoor/outdoor aspect of the house. It's so versatile—there are lots of different spaces I can use. The pattern is right for the way I live, and great for entertaining."

Acorn's concern for energy efficiency shows up in the variety of solar heating systems it offers, in the care it takes in constructing its wall panels, in the quality of its door and window components, and in the extensive insulation package it includes in each kit. Because their steep-pitched roofs make Acorn

This model has both a solarium and an enclosed porch.

Mary Catherwood's home from the Independence Series.

Opposite page: Even the bathroom of an Acorn home is sunny and spacious.

The Independence 1500 includes three bedrooms and a full basement.

homes particularly well-suited to active solar heating systems, the company offers its own Sunwave system to all of its customers. Acorn and Raytheon Corp. developed the Sunwave system as a joint venture, with assistance from the U.S. Department of Energy. Acorn recommends that the system be used primarily for heating water, since this accounts for a good third of the energy bill in any house.

Acorn designs and manufactures wall panels for its houses with an eye toward maximizing energy efficiency. Pre-

assembled in a controlled environment according to rigorous standards of quality, the panels are much less likely to swell, crack, or buckle when exposed to the elements than those of conventionally built homes, resulting in a tighter house.

In addition to manufacturing wall panels, Acorn provides excellent energy-saving door and window components, such as Pella wood casement and awning windows with low-emissivity glass; Pella steel-clad insulating core doors; French double-door sets and insulated skylights; and Peachtree wood sliding glass doors.

Acorn takes great care in insulating all its homes. Besides supplying rigid foam insulation for the roof, walls and floor, Acorn also includes in each kit such energy-saving features as Du Pont Tyvek building wrap to protect against air and moisture infiltration; Dow Sill Seal R foam rolls for sill insulation; foam gaskets at the electrical outlets; high-adhesion sealing tape on the vapor/infiltration barrier; and a flashing kit for use on the chimney/roof vapor barrier joint.

The superior insulation package and passive solar design of Mary Catherwood's house combine to reduce her energy bills. Mary explains, "Even with electrical heat and hot water—which is, relatively speaking, more expensive

A multi-level interior provides attractive, comfortable living spaces.

than gas or oil—my energy bill averages $1000 for twelve months."

All the building materials Acorn supplies are top grade, from the #1 Douglas fir beams and posts for the floor system; to Western red cedar vertical siding or horizontal clapboards for the exterior; to stairs, detailing, and interior doors of clear stain-grade red oak. The interior options include a choice of satin chrome or brass-finish hardware, and Western red cedar interior paneling, which customers can select in place of drywall.

Fieldstone fireplaces and built-in shelves add a cozy touch.

> "*All the materials Acorn supplies are good to excellent in quality. . . . Acorn gives you a really nicely finished house,*" says a satisfied Connecticut homeowner.

Mary really appreciates this kind of attention to detail in her own home. In fact, it was one of the factors that helped her decide to buy an Acorn home. "Before I started, I talked pretty carefully with other Acorn owners. One who had acted as his own general contractor impressed me with the fact that all the materials Acorn supplies are good to excellent in quality. I really wanted to be sure I wasn't being taken for a ride in that respect. I also took resale value into con-

sideration. Acorn gives you a really nicely finished house. It was not inexpensive, so I wanted to be sure about liking the details."

Because Acorn uses such high-quality materials in manufacturing its houses, the cost of an Acorn home runs relatively high. Of course, Acorn customers don't pay as much for the materials as they would if they built on their own, because the company purchases in bulk

Sunspaces adjoin the master bedroom and living and dining rooms in the Independence 2000.

at a discount and passes the savings along. But because its kits can cost more than some buyers might be able to afford, Acorn offers two types of house packages.

The Full Finish package, the more expensive of the two alternatives, consists of a completely finished, ready-to-move-into home that has all mechanical systems installed, a full kitchen, finished trim throughout, and finish flooring installed—a real turnkey home. The price for a Full Finish version of Acorn's smallest stock model, the 850-square-foot Nutshell Farmstead, ranges from $70,000 to $80,000.

By contrast, if a buyer purchased the same house under the second plan—the Erected Shell—sold by Acorn, it would cost between $40,000 and $50,000.

Steep-pitched roofs make Acorn homes particularly well-suited to active solar heating systems.

Acorn designs adapt well to wooded sites.

Acorn markets the Erected Shell package as a less expensive alternative for those who want to save money by handling some or all of their own mechanical or contracting work. Erected Shells offer the most impressive savings for customers who buy the larger Acorn kits. For instance, a 3,600-square-foot Country House costs $280,000 to $300,000 fully finished, compared to $180,000 to $200,000 for just the shell. ∎

Each Acorn house package contains:

- A floor system of #1 pre-cut Douglas fir posts and beams
- Kiln-dried Western hem-fir pre-cut joists
- Premium-grade underlayment tongue and groove plywood for the subfloor, also pre-cut and supplied with glue
- Factory-assembled exterior wall panels of kiln-dried Western hem-fir framing, with plywood interior sheathing
- Pella wood casement and awning windows, low-emissivity insulating glass fixed windows
- Pressure-treated yellow pine sills
- Western red cedar vertical siding or horizontal clapboards
- Pella steel-clad insulating core exterior doors, Peachtree wood sliding glass doors, Pella French double-doors sets; optional mahogany or cherry entry doors
- Pre-cut Douglas fir post and beam roof system and decking
- Pre-cut Western hem-fir posts and railings with pine balusters
- Interior partitions of kiln-dried Western hem-fir studs, pre-cut
- Interior stairs of clear stain-grade solid red oak
- Pre-hung interior doors of red oak in clear pine jambs with satin chrome hardware
- Clear pine trim on doors, baseboards, and windows
- All hardware necessary for construction
- All-wood pre-finished cabinets for kitchen and bath
- Energy-saving insulation package

Lots of windows let the sun shine in.

ADIRONDACK ALTERNATE ENERGY

A custom-designed, energy-efficient home from Adirondack Alternate Energy.

For a practically maintenance-free home built to maintain a comfortable, even interior temperature throughout the cold season, consider the houses offered by Adirondack Alternate Energy. Originally designed as vacation homes for part-time residents of New York's Adirondack Mountains, AAE houses now provide pleasant year-round living for people who want to save money on their energy bills. "We built our house in 1984," says Charlie Markarian of Patterson, New York. "We had been considering an alternative lifestyle, and the idea of having minimal energy costs and being able to spend our money on other things really appealed to us. We did a lot of investigation into the topic, and AAE seemed the best way to go. They had done more research on their houses than others, and really seemed to know more about what was going on."

Adirondack Alternate Energy designs each of its Low Energy Requirement (LER) houses to incorporate four ele-

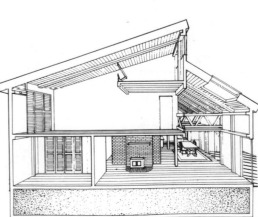

Section diagram shows Heat Energy Battery at base of house and passive solar design.

ments it considers essential to maximum energy efficiency: insulation, south-facing glass, a thermal mass, and a special air-handling system. Its integrated approach to passive solar design results in houses that maintain even, comfortable interior temperatures. The AAE insulation envelope surrounds each house on all six sides with rigid board cellular foam insulation. Installed both above and below ground, the unbroken weather seal has an average rating of R-36.

AAE helps homeowners orient their houses to within 15 degrees of true south in order that south-facing windows admit the greatest possible amount of sunlight. By designing south walls to incorporate 30% glass, installing double-glazed windows on south, east, and west faces, and using high performance glass in any windows on the north side, AAE ensures that its LER houses get three times as much solar energy as they need. This eliminates the potential for large temperature swings.

Every LER home includes a thermal mass consisting of about 200 tons of sand or concrete. Transfer ducts in the mass connect a central plenum (in the form of a chimney) to registers at the perimeter of the house. Powered by one or two small fans, air circulates through the mass, up through the house, and then down through the chimney back into the storage bed. The company refers to this heat exchange system as a Heat Energy Battery (HEB). Whenever air in the house is warmer than the thermal mass, the mass absorbs energy, and whenever the house is cooler than the storage medium, heat radiates back into the air. Just like a car battery, the HEB continually charges and discharges.

It may sound far too simple, but it really works. According to Dr. Lawrence Smith of Orangeville, Pennsylvania, who built an AAE LER home in 1982, "This past winter was our fifth in the house, and we just become more pleased every year. We only have to use the wood stove every three to four days, and we used less than a cord of wood last winter. AAE has a really terrific idea — most people don't believe you can get away with a passive solar home in the northeast, but this house sure proves them wrong. We

The elegant interior of an AAE home has lots of windows to gather warmth and light from the sun.

Top: Rigid foam board insulation covers the exterior of the house.

Bottom left: Ample south-facing glass and saltbox design contribute to energy efficiency.

Bottom right: AAE houses rely on tight construction to enhance energy efficiency.

have a massive heat storage system," Larry continues, "with a 300-ton thermal mass—220 tons of crushed limestone dust, which is dense and highly compactible, very suitable as a storage medium, and 80 tons of concrete. The thermal mass works so well that it took two winters to finish burning the scraps of wood left over from building the house! That's how infrequently we use the wood stove. When the sun shines you don't need to light it. On a bright day in January, we have to keep the windows open so we don't get too hot."

Charlie Markarian describes a similar experience. "Last winter we used less than a cord of wood. It's unbelievable how the house maintains a steady inte-

---

"*W*e only have to use the wood stove every three to four days, and we used less than a cord of wood last winter," says an AAE owner.

---

rior temperature at all times—it's like magic. There's never more than a ten-degree temperature swing in a twenty-four-hour period, no matter what's going on outside."

By conducting energy research and experimenting with actual homes since the mid-1970s, AAE has arrived at a de-

The Heat Energy Battery circulates air throughout the house.

sign approach that takes into account the body heat generated by a house's inhabitants as they go about their daily activities, and employs it as a source of heat. Many designers of super-insulated homes fail to take body heat into consideration when planning houses, and as a result the houses can become uncomfortably overheated. AAE's design avoids this pitfall.

AAE's tightly sealed, well-insulated homes offer a side benefit in the form of a high level of interior humidity. "My wife has dry skin, but with a 40–50 percent humidity level (the optimum comfort level) she doesn't have any trouble with winter itchiness. It's great for the plants, too. It's a moist heat, so you don't have to use a humidifier," says Charlie.

The Markarians also found AAE's free design service appealing. AAE sells only custom homes, and offers no stock plans. It designs every house especially for the site and the owners. "They do all the design and engineering drawings for you, and they don't charge extra," says Charlie. "They have a formula for the ratio of south-facing glass per square foot of interior space, and they do the architectural design and the engineering together—that makes the house energy-efficient and good-looking at the same time. The AAE designers spend a lot of time talking to you. They get ideas and input from you on your life-style so they can design your home to suit you. It wasn't just a question of how many bedrooms; it was more abstract than that.

"My wife wanted a house that would eventually accommodate a family," Charlie adds, "but right now we both work, so it had to be designed to accommodate two people who would be away a lot to begin with. In terms of more concrete problems, we wanted a kind of combination kitchen/dining room, since everyone ends up in the kitchen anyway. We wanted a place where everyone could get together and relax. What we got is a house that's very comfortable and casual. Not only is it well-suited to our current life-style, it's beautifully

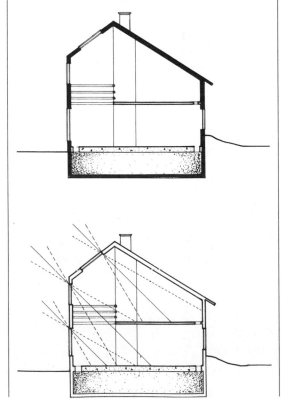

sited, with a terrific view of the Berkshires."

In addition to its design service, AAE also supplies technical assistance throughout the construction process. "We want to remain very close to our customers," says AAE president Bruce Brownell. "We become friends with them, we talk with them long after the sale. A unique thing about our company is that when the materials hit the site and we've been paid, we're only beginning to do business with people. We don't say, 'Have a good time, build your house, so long.'" AAE's construction assistance includes site visits and two or three telephone calls per week from a company representative, continuing for

Above: AAE interiors can be casual or formal as desired.

Far left: Solar diagram shows how sunlight penetrates the home's interior to provide warmth at different times of the year.

a year or more after AAE first delivers the material.

"Dealing with AAE was a tremendous saving of time and labor over a stick-built home," says Larry Smith. "Everything came on one trailer and there was no running around. It was very efficient. AAE provided a lot of technical supervision and made three or four on-site visits, checking to make sure everything was all right. We were in constant contact with them, too, talking every two or three days. I acted as a site boss, the liaison between AAE and the framing crew—it was fun for me to come to understand and participate in the building process."

The close supervision provided by AAE saved Charlie Markarian's home from near disaster. "We had trouble with the builder. He wasn't paying close enough attention to getting all the details right. In fact we had to fire him, because he didn't put the insulation in properly, and this house has to be insulated very carefully. It's very, very important. When Bruce Brownell came and looked at the house on his inspection and took me aside and said that the insulation was put in so sloppily it was nearly ineffectual, we were really worried that our dream was going down the tubes. But it didn't happen. I ended up acting as the general contractor and

A saltbox design from AAE has a wraparound deck and a tower room.

doing the rest of the work myself. AAE was really helpful and recommended subcontractors who were really good people. Everything went fine after that."

You can build your AAE house using either post and beam or conventional framing. Since it custom-designs each house, AAE does not provide a price list, but it does quote examples like the following: A two-story, 2,240-square-foot saltbox house, with 3 bedrooms, 2 full baths, kitchen, dining room, and cathedral ceilinged great room represents a typical AAE house. If it includes some interior pine paneling, Andersen ter-

> *"A unique thing about our company is that when the materials hit the site and we've been paid, we're only beginning to do business with our customers," says AAE's president.*

retone casement windows, and exterior verticle pine siding, and has a partial post and beam frame, the house shell package would cost about $44,500.

In addition to the shell, AAE customers buying a house like this saltbox invest an average $9,263 in the HEB package. Owners acting as their own general contractors could complete the shell and HEB—obtaining plumbing, electrical, and masonry elsewhere, and

adding an interior air handling system — for another $40,974. With all interior finishing, the total cost of the house would come to about $123,000, not including foundation. AAE will, at the customer's request, supply an optional foundation package for $10,000.

"We like the house because it's simple, not high-tech, and yet it works very well," says Larry Smith. "The house is really very efficient. We're still working our way through the woodpile. We're really happy. In fact, we like it so much we'd build another one!" ▪

AAE Low Energy Requirement house packages contain all of the construction materials to build the HEB and shell, including:

- □ **LER package:** all framing materials, for post and beam or conventional house; all interior subfloors and partitions; windows and doors; all insulation and sealing materials
- □ **HEB package:** insulated storage medium for sand or concrete; aluminum air transfer ducts
- □ **Fans and motors for air-handling system**

A two-story home on a sloping site offers additional living space in a single story wing.

Opposite page: The air-circulation pipes for the Heat Energy Battery are put in place before the sand-concrete mass is poured.

AFFORDABLE LUXURY HOMES

According to Betsy and Ray Williams of Louisville, Kentucky, "We were in the process of thinking about building a new home when our sister-in-law told us about a house under construction in Lexington. The owner, a research physicist, had investigated thirty-five house manufacturers before he had decided to buy his house from Affordable Luxury Homes. Intrigued by the story, we went to see the house. We were so impressed by the high quality of materials and carpentry that we decided to buy a home of our own from Affordable."

Top & bottom: Affordable offers both contemporary and traditional designs.

Founded in the mid 1970s, Affordable Luxury Homes manufactures high-quality panelized houses in literally any size, shape, or form. The company does 90 percent of its business in custom-designed homes, many of which customers order through the mail and over the phone. Buyers can choose from Affordable's many stock models and mod-

ify the one they select, or send the company floor plans—or even a rough sketch—and it will design their home. Affordable's house staff of architects and engineers can design many different types of homes, both traditional and contemporary, including passive solar.

Ray and Betsy had already had plans drawn up for them by an architect when they found out about ALH. "We sent

> *"The houses are much tighter and truer than stick-built houses," says one owner. "The panels are amazingly strong."*

them to Affordable for the initial estimate," the Williams note. "They can give you a fairly accurate price 'guestimate' from your own plans and specs. Then, if you have them design a house for you, the design fee runs about $0.50 per square foot. They will tell you exactly how much that's going to cost. They're very good about that. Then if you build within twelve months of having the plans drawn up, the fee applies to the cost of the house—like a deposit. It's really quite reasonable."

Affordable offers about thirty stock homes that represent a wide range of styles and sizes. The Clear Creek Chalet model, an A-frame with 1,650 square feet, offers a downstairs master bed-

room, two upstairs bedrooms, a family room with sliding glass doors to the outside, two baths, and a kitchen with a pantry. A fireplace, two-story ceiling, and outside deck highlight the spacious living room. The standard model comes with the energy-efficient 6-inch panelized roof system.

The more traditional Continental fea-

Top & bottom: Homes from Affordable are ideally suited for family living.

tures a substantial amount of living space—almost 2,900 square feet on two floors. This colonial includes four bedrooms, an attached garage, two full baths, and two half-baths. Another two-story model in traditional styling, the Madrid, offers a sophisticated passive solar heating system that makes use of the six-inch panelized roof package and a solarium. Occupying 1,777 square feet, this home has three bedrooms, two baths, and an attached garage.

Buyers have a wide range of options that can turn even a stock house into a personal design.

Affordable puts together its kits so that buyers have a wide range of options that can turn even a stock house into a personal design. At an additional cost, buyers can choose such items as cedar shake shingles, aluminum-clad wood-frame windows, 6-inch panel construction, plumbing fixtures, kitchen cabinets, and even custom-built sunrooms and greenhouses.

Affordable builds its wall panels to precise standards; inspectors permit a tolerance factor of only ⅟₃₂ inch to assure everything fits together as designed. Panel construction involves several steps. The sophisticated manufacturing process starts with the lamination of

many thin layers of wood to form rigid sheets of plywood. Affordable's factory workers build panel frames with 2×4 lumber, apply the exterior sheathing, install electrical wiring and outlet boxes, lay in expanded polystyrene foam, cut the drywall, apply adhesive, and laminate all parts of the sandwich under great pressure to form one very strong piece.

"Affordable makes them very well," explains Ray. "The houses are tighter and truer than stick-built houses. The panels are amazingly strong. When Af-

Top: This model makes use of clerestory windows and a solarium for passive solar heating.

Bottom: This traditional dining room fits right in.

A row of dormers and a columned porch add to this home's appeal.

fordable's crew built our house, they had to cut a hole in the roof for the chimney. They couldn't do it beforehand because it has to be absolutely accurate. They had such a hard time cutting through the roof panel—they almost couldn't do it. It was astonishing how tough it was."

Affordable's homes have other, equally impressive features. The company uses no highly inflammable or toxic products in the standard package construction. (The polystyrene, for example, will not burn.) Home components meet or exceed all building codes; Indiana state (the company is based in Markle, Indiana) or third-party inspectors check each item. Homes come with 200-amp electrical

service. Factory workers apply drywall panels with self-tapping screws, rather than nails. They place moisture-resistant insulation behind all tubs and showers on exterior walls. And company engineers make individual structural calculations for each home ordered to insure structural integrity.

Owners must build the foundation to the same precision-engineered standards the company uses for the rest of the house, since Affordable's crew can't compensate for a poor foundation while erecting the panels. This step requires a do-it-yourselfer with extensive foundation experience or a masonry contractor. The buyer chooses the type of founda-

Several steps of house construction in the factory.

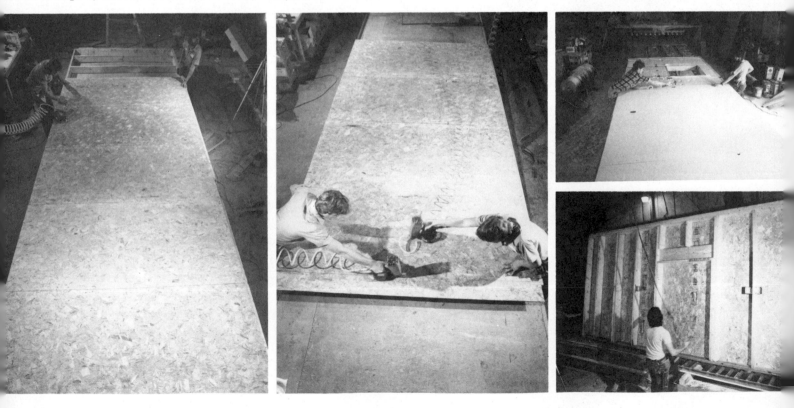

tion, but must build it before the panels arrive.

Affordable Luxury Homes offers several levels of construction assistance, from on-site supervision to a complete turnkey package. The Williams chose to buy only an erected shell, opting to finish their home themselves. "We were extremely impressed with the crew that Affordable supplied," says Ray. "They did all the work at an amazingly low price, and they were such nice people. They knew exactly what to do and did it with care and pride. They built the house like a fort."

The panels arrive at the construction site on a truck loaded so that the crew can take them off in the order they're needed. A crane sets the panels in place on site, and the crew goes to work bolting them down. The crew assembles the exterior shell first, then installs the interior partitions. Affordable's careful attention to detail, especially in lap joints where corners fit together and butt joints where two panels meet, ensures that every component fits together without gaps. Ray was very impressed with the flexibility of the panelized method:

"Anything you can do with a stick-built house, you can do with one of these — faster, easier, and better."

With the first and second floors in place, the crew builds the roof to complete the shell. Depending on the design of the house, the crew uses either roof trusses or ceiling/roof panels to construct the roof. The process of erecting

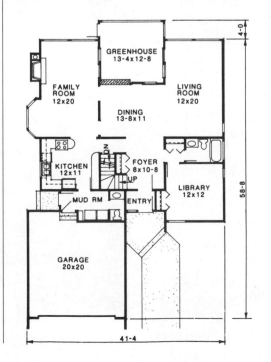

107

the shell takes about one working day. The time factor has financial advantages as well. Since the structure goes up in only a few days, owners can keep ahead of their construction loans. The crew closes in the house in a short period of time, so the bank can provide the next draw to start paying the subcontractors. Affordable's method of construction permits subcontractors to start quickly on the inside and be out of the wind. In this way, buyers can build houses all year round. The timetable is guaranteed, the cost is fixed, and there are no unpleasant surprises.

Ray has nothing but praise for the company. "The people at Affordable are really honest and sincere—you can trust them," he states. "They were very easy to deal with, too. In fact, we're grateful to them for being so flexible on the money required as a deposit on the house plans. We didn't have quite enough money for the full deposit, so they accepted what we could pay them, and started construction anyway. They seemed more concerned about keeping us happy! They're typically Midwestern—so honest it hurts. It's really a family business, and everyone cares about it. You get really good services and an abundance of good materials—what more could you ask?"

Since most people alter even the stock models, the final price of a home depends on several variables. And buyers who do the finishing work themselves can save up to 50 percent of the cost of subcontracting. The Clear Creek Chalet has a price of $28,000 for the basic package and costs around $36,000 to complete, if the owner does the finishing. The Continental runs $29,000 for the basic pack-

On Site, a crane drops the panels into place on the foundation.

age and $42,000 to complete. Homes can cost considerably more, depending on the options, special design features, and fixtures chosen. Affordable also offers several services, including financing and subcontracting.

Company president Karol Cossairt is proud of the design, engineering, and support services his company offers. "No one else does what we do," he says. "And because we work with people from all over the United States, we have a lot of fun doing it." ■

Customers can choose horizontal or vertical siding.

The Standard Basic Package includes:

- Nominal 4-inch closed panels with polystyrene insulation; ⁷/₁₆-inch waferboard exterior sheathing; and ½-inch gypsum wallboard interior sheathing
- Pre-framed 2 × 4 interior wall panels or materials for on-site construction, depending on design
- Second-floor framing system with ¾-inch tongue and groove sheathing subfloor
- 2 × 6 subfascia
- Roof system with trusses: sheathing, fiberglass shingles, felt paper, nails, metal drip edge, and ply clips. For homes with panelized roof construction: framing, sheathing, insulation, drywall for ceiling, fiberglass shingles, felt paper, roofing nails, metal drip edge.
- Aluminum dual-pane windows and patio doors, with screens
- Stanley insulated steel exterior doors

- Air infiltration system, including foam sill sealer and spray foam
- Roof vents, soffit vents, and aluminum valley flashing, depending on design
- Stanley garage door, depending on design
- 4-inch open panels for garage, depending on design
- Pre-cut stairway package, depending on design
- Nails and fasteners
- Loose lumber for on-site bracing, etc.
- Gable end sheathing, depending on design
- Porch beams and posts, depending on design
- Plans and design work necessary for construction
- On-site placement of wall, ceiling, and roof panels

The company offers a video tape about the Affordable building method, and another tape on home financing.

FARWEST HOMES

Farwest Homes offers several single-family home designs to customers in the Pacific Northwest, Alaska, and Hawaii, including one-story, split-level, and two-story houses in both contemporary and traditional styles. The company uses panelized wall components constructed of 2 × 4 framing, insulation, drywall, and a choice of exterior finishes, including cedar, plywood, and hardboard. Factory workers install all windows and door frames to simplify on-site work. Farwest offers such optional features and services as wood-frame windows, aluminum triple-glazed windows, 2 × 6 framing, balconies and sun decks, custom designs, and construction supervision.

The three-bedroom Westerner provides 1,230 square feet of living space in

a ranch style. Distinctive features include a 20 × 15-foot living room, separate dining area, attached garage, and two baths. The whole house occupies a compact 48 × 50-foot area. The larger Eldorado design encompasses four bedrooms, a family room, an eat-in kitchen, a patio, and a front-entrance courtyard—for a total of 2,650 square feet on one level.

In the two-level Berkshire, vaulted ceilings highlight the great room and master bedroom, which also has its own bathroom. A covered porch, breakfast nook, window seat in the foyer, and two upstairs bedrooms complete this unique house, which offers 1,103 square feet on the main floor and 486 square feet on the upper floor. The Sunridge, which has 2,508 square feet on two levels, offers a master bedroom with a bathroom, walk-in closet, dressing area, and deck. The cathedral ceiling rises above both the 154-square-foot dining room and the 310-square-foot living room, which also has a deck. A fourth bedroom and a 24-foot-long recreation room occupy the lower level. ■

The basic package for a stock model contains:

- Assembled exterior wall panels; door frames and glazed window units, installed
- Assembled gables with siding
- Assembled roof trusses
- ½-inch exterior plywood roof sheathing
- Fascia and miscellaneous moldings
- Assembled interior partitions with door and closet headers, installed
- Aluminum windows and sliding doors, with screens
- Primed metal exterior doors
- Garage doors
- Interior doors, pre-hung in jambs
- Bi-folding wardrobe doors

Top: Panels are simply lowered into place on site.

Middle: Panels under construction in the factory.

Left: This adaptation of the Mountaineer II has an alpine look.

MARLEY CONTINENTAL HOMES

W e bought our Uni-Structure as an investment," notes Marcia Aptt of Gloucester, Massachusetts, of her Marley module house. "It's a single-family house with a split foyer, and we adapted the plan to make it a two-family house. We finished off the downstairs as a separate apartment. We built the foundation off the ground so there's a full basement with windows and daylight. My husband travels a lot, and we both really are busy, so we needed to choose something that went up quickly. We also wanted to have rental income start coming in as soon as possible. We had a tenant for the upstairs apartment within six weeks. It was an excellent way to build a two-family investment home.

"We wanted it to look like a single-family residence, and that was very easy to do. Of course, Marley also sells multi-unit residential buildings, but most of those were bigger than what we wanted. I think this would be a very good thing for a young couple to do—build a house like this, make it a two-family residence, live in one part and rent out the other, so they would have an income to help pay for the house. And then eventually, they could convert it to a single family house when it was all paid for."

Founded in 1954 as a conglomerate of several smaller companies, and now one of the nation's larger home producers, Marley operates four factories: Nashua, New

This house built by Marley Continental Homes doesn't look like it came out of a factory.

Opposite page: Marley offers many choices for interior finishing throughout the house.

112

Hampshire; Roanoake, Virginia; Haines City, Florida; and Osage City, Kansas. Each factory can produce sixty homes a week — an impressive number, considering that some manufacturers don't sell that many in a year.

The New Hampshire plant ships to the six New England states and New York. The Virginia plant takes care of the Mid-Atlantic region, the Florida plant has the South, and the Kansas plant covers the Midwest and West.

> *Uni-Structure houses offer a variety of exterior styles and interior decor, and arrive 90 percent complete.*

Marley sells both the Uni-Structure modular house and panelized houses, which customers can have built with their choice of floor plan and style. Modular homes, like the panelized structures, are factory-built, but come more completely finished.

The Uni-Structure line offers a variety of exterior styles and interior decor in houses that arrive from the manufacturer 90 percent complete, outfitted down to the carpeting, plumbing, and wallpaper, with a standard electric range and other optional appliances already installed. Houses usually reach the building site in two sections, each loaded on

the back of a tractor-trailer. A crane unloads the sections and swings them into place on the foundation. Marley calls this method "pre-site building." Using this type of construction helps control costs, eliminating the expenses that can be caused by weather delays or supply shortages. In addition, by constructing each house before shipping it, the manufacturer can guarantee that the building will match the specs exactly.

People choose Uni-Structure homes for a variety of reasons. Bob Driscoll of Lawrence, Kansas, had a parcel of land he sought to develop, and he wanted a smaller house he could use as a retirement home. "A friend of mine who worked for a builder recommended a Uni-Structure home, and it was a good choice," he says. "Right now I'm renting it to one of my in-laws, but I plan to move in when I retire. I've been living in the same house for twenty years—a big old house that my grandchildren come to visit in. At the moment, I need the space!"

For Sandra Hughes and her husband, of Portsmouth, New Hampshire, building costs were a prime concern. "We selected our house on the basis of cost and quality," she says. "We already owned the land. We were moving back into the state after several years in Georgia. We looked at other types of modular houses, but the plan for this model came closest to what we wanted. This is the third house that we built ourselves. We built the first one in Portsmouth, and the second was in

This contemporary design has a shed roof and single-story wing.

Two halves of a Uni-Structure in the factory, before exterior siding goes on.

Georgia. Then, when we moved back here, we decided to try a modular home. The cost of housing is very high in this area. We couldn't afford to buy land and build a house from scratch."

Marley builds homes from kiln-dried, grade-marked lumber, starting with the subfloor, which it nails and glues to eliminate squeaks. Workers roll the floor covering into place and join the floor system to the pre-assembled wall system. They set interior and exterior walls into place during the same process and nail them down. The house module then continues down the assembly line for the addition of other components.

Factory workers install the electrical wiring in the pre-routed floor chase, a technique that reduces air leaks. They also caulk around all structural openings. As the electrical wiring goes in, the plumbing also nears completion, with pre-assembled and tested units in place. Upon completion of the wiring and plumbing, construction has taken between 14 and 18 hours to reach a point that a site-built house achieves in a minimum of two weeks.

Workers then paint the exterior and seal all joints with caulking. Marley's own inspectors and an independent third party check everything at least five times and sign cards attached to each part indicating that it has passed the rigorous examination.

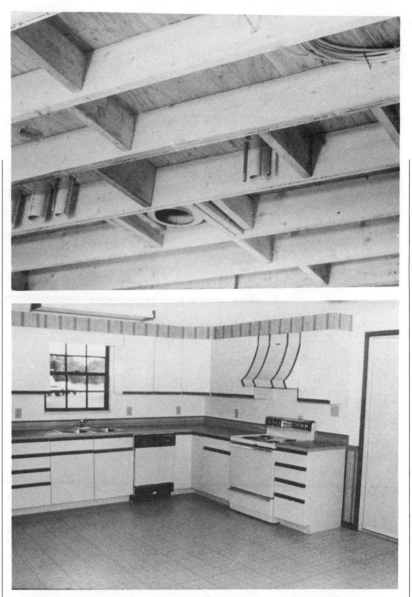

Twenty-five hours after the first step, modules enter the finish assembly line, where workers tack down the ceiling insulation and test the plumbing system for water tightness. They complete all finish work on the doors, including jambs, trim, and hardware; and they install kitchen cabinets and hang the wallpaper. Finally, with everything in place, they give the house a thorough cleaning and secure cabinet doors and appliances for the trip to the site.

The manufacturer uses a special type of hinged roof truss that folds down during transport. The company also hinges the eaves to keep the module narrow enough to fit on the trailer.

Marley covers the house to protect the exterior and interior from the elements during shipping. Inside, the purchaser

Top: Marley uses only high-grade materials in the construction of its homes.

Middle: All Uni-Structure modular homes come with a complete kitchen already installed.

Left: This design features an attached two-car garage.

will find everything needed to finish the home, including caulking, shutters, nails, pre-cut lumber, and other items. The whole production process takes about ninety-six hours.

"The crew lifted the house off the trailer with a crane and put the two halves together," says Marcia Aptt of the arrival of her home. "Then they raised the roof up to form the peak. It was shipped folded down like a doll's house. They applied the siding on-site, although sometimes they do that in the factory. Our house arrived with rugs loosely laid, and they had cut them precisely to fit. Everything was very good quality, and we had no trouble getting the house finished and ready for tenants to move into."

Bob Driscoll took three months to finish his home. "I never even considered hiring a builder, I did it all myself," he says. "I found the whole process to be a very good experience and I'm quite pleased with the house."

Marley offers over eighty models of flexible single-family modular homes, including the Expand-a-Home series—basic houses that owners can add to as

families and incomes grow. Styles range from a modest traditional Cape Cod to a sleek, contemporary solar home. The Uni-Structure allows great freedom in developing a highly individual design. Customers can match floor plans with different exteriors. Similarly, they can pick interior details to meet personal tastes and requirements.

"We made a lot of changes on our three-bedroom, two-bath Laredo model Uni-Structure," says Sandra Hughes. "We knocked out some walls. We also

Top left: A sweeping curved staircase is one interior option.

Above and below: Marley offers commercial and multi-tenant models in addition to single-family homes.

Opposite page: This "prefab" house has bow windows and a front porch for a Victorian look.

Top: Marley offers a variety of exterior designs, including contemporary.

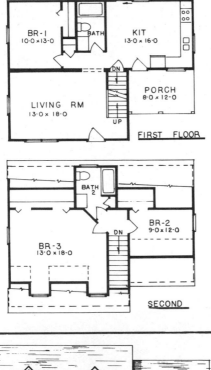

FIRST FLOOR

BR-1
10-0 × 13-0

BATH

KIT
13-0 × 16-0

DN

LIVING RM
13-0 × 18-0

PORCH
8-0 × 12-0

UP

SECOND

BATH 2

BR-3
13-0 × 18-0

DN

BR-2
9-0 × 12-0

Right: The Heather Cottage is a two-bedroom cape.

installed French doors that lead out to a terrace, which wasn't in the original plan. We changed the kitchen and opened up the archways between the living room and the dining room. Marley was very good about letting us sit down and change things on the interior. It's harder to alter the main lines of the house, but changing the inside was not difficult."

Marley's own inspectors and an independent third party must check everything at least five times before a house can pass their rigorous examination.

Marcia agrees. "I find both the interior and the exterior of our Uni-Structure house attractive and easy to maintain. Another thing that we liked about Marley is that they offered us about eight or ten choices of wallpaper and linoleum, so it was easy to come to a decision. The light fixtures, too, are all very attractive—we are very pleased."

Marley Continental sells its houses through hundreds of authorized builder-dealers throughout the country. The builders set prices according to whatever level of completion the customer desires. Therefore, Marley does not publish a price list. Prospective customers can obtain estimated prices from the nearest local dealer. ■

A Marley living room can even include a fireplace.

A Marley Continental Homes modular home package contains the following pre-assembled items:

- Floor framing and subfloor girders, joists, subflooring and bridging
- Walls with 2 × 4 studding, shoe plate and top plate, with headers as shown on plans
- Exterior sheathing of ½-inch plywood, with optional waferboard
- Roof trusses, factory-installed, with 4 5/12-pitch roof for 24-foot and 26-foot-wide models, and 4/12-pitch roof for 28-foot-wide models
- Site-installed roof framing for two-story models
- Roof-sheathing of ½-inch plywood, with waferboard and 5/8-inch plywood optional
- 240 lb. 12 × 36 Sealtab roof shingles over 15-lb. asphalt felt on factory-installed roofs
- Standard exterior siding of primed masonite lap. Other sidings, including vinyl, optional
- Windows of Crestline insulated glass, wood-framed and triple-glazed
- Insulated steel exterior doors
- Interior doors of masonite hollow core pre-finished wood grain
- Hardwood, pre-finished cove colonial base, window and door trim
- Wood or metal closet rods

- Exterior trim
- Ventilation louvers and vents
- Interior finish of ½-inch gypsum on walls and ceiling, factory finished
- Wall finish of off-white latex paint
- Vinyl wallpaper in kitchen, halls, and baths
- Kitchen cabinets
- General Electric kitchen appliances, range standard; dishwasher, refrigerator, and oven, optional
- Washer/dryer available as option
- Combination hood/light/vent for stove
- Smoke detector
- Garbage disposal
- Basement, second floor, and split-entry stairways
- Kitchen sink: stainless steel, double-bowl, with single lever faucet
- All fixtures for main bath, half-bath, and three-quarter bath
- Factory-installed electric baseboard heating, or hot water baseboard heating, with oil or gas boiler optional
- Main electrical panel box, outlets, and switches, installed
- All insulation, factory installed, to R-30 on ceilings (R-38 optional); R-13 for exterior walls, and R-11 under the first floor
- Inlaid vinyl flooring in kitchen and bath
- Nylon carpet over all other floors
- All nails, fasteners, locksets, etc.

MILES HOMES

Miles Homes has a network of representatives all over the country. These dealers can help customers work out homebuilding problems of all kinds, from finding a site to financing their house, to deciding how involved they want to be in construction. The company offers a custom design service, so that customers can modify the interior and exterior of their house to suit themselves—adding, subtracting, or changing the shapes of rooms, or even changing the overall size of their house. To make the design process easier, Miles provides CAD services as well.

Since Miles is a division of Insilco, a large corporation, it can offer financial packages that many smaller companies cannot. Customers can buy a complete

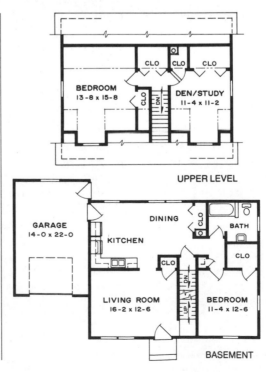

Top: The 1,142-square-foot Fairfield model offers two bedrooms, with room for expansion.

Left: The Morgan offers living on two levels, with two bedrooms and a den/study.

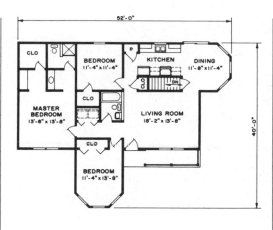

home package from Miles and receive significant financial help based on their land ownership and their sweat equity participation in the project. Miles financial packages feature:

- No-down-payment construction financing on materials
- Below-market interest rates
- Deferred monthly payments
- Foundation and framing financial assistance
- Credit on finishing packages bought from Miles

Miles offers thirty-eight standard home models, plus its eleven Pathway Collection models, a group of lower-cost homes specifically designed for easy do-it-yourself construction. For customers who decide to build their homes themselves, the company runs construction seminars in addition to providing instruction manuals and video tapes.

Prices for Miles Basic Homes Packages range from $25,200 for an 823-square-foot home to $64,500 for one twice as big. The less expensive Pathway models cost between $23,200 and $34,400.

Miles Basic Homes Packages include everything except kitchen cabinets, paint, heating supplies, plumbing supplies, electrical supplies, carpeting, floor tiles, light fixtures, and bathroom accessories. ∎

Top left: The Tyler has three bedrooms and a dining ell.

Top right: Miles offers a choice of both contemporary and traditional exteriors.

Left: Do-it-yourself homebuilders can save money on a Miles home.

NORTHERN HOMES

Northern Homes has built 30,000 homes since its founding in 1946. The company produces traditional and contemporary homes in any style, size, and design customers request, as long as the houses are wood frame and structurally sound. In addition to conventional single-family housing, Northern builds dome homes, commercial structures, and multi-family housing. By tailoring each package to meet customers' time and budget needs as well as their tastes, Northern helps clients save money in reduced labor costs, waste, and interest charges.

Northern Homes selects the materials and components for its houses with great care, right down to the last nail. To reduce waste and further guarantee quality, the company re-grades all lumber and materials at its factory. While components such as Andersen windows and Peachtree doors meet Northern's strict criteria, the company manufactures many items itself whenever those produced elsewhere do not measure up to its standards.

Customers have a multitude of options when planning their Northern home. They can choose from ten different colors of fiberglass roof shingles, as well as wood shingles. Northern offers many types of siding, including spruce, five kinds of cedar, two kinds of pine, aluminum, and vinyl. Windows come in a variety of styles (including circular and

The Bedford features a Dutch Colonial exterior and a spacious interior with three bedrooms.

The Hampton Bays, from Northern Homes' Contemporary Collection, offers an outdoor deck and 1,400 square feet of living space.

oblong) as do interior and exterior doors: Northern offers six stock colonial entrances that customers can adapt for double or single doors, sidelights, and toplights. Interior doors come in hollow or solid core birch, six-panel hardboard or pine, full- or top-louvered, lauan, or oak. The company also manufactures custom doors in its shop.

Northern's standard models fall into three architectural categories: colonial, contemporary, and traditional. Reflecting authentic colonial design elements, Northern's line of colonials—the Americana Collection—offers homes that range in size from the 1,432-square-foot Newbury to the 3,508-square-foot Ethan Allen. The Ethan Allen includes a sun room, wet and dry pantries, and complete private guest or maid's quarters, along with four bedrooms, three and a half baths, and a living room, dining room, kitchen, breakfast room, and two-car garage.

Homes from Northern's Contemporary Collection start at 1,220 square feet and range up to 2,658 square feet. These models include a variety of roof lines, such as shed roofs and prows, and incorporate skylights, vaulted ceilings, open plan interiors, and other such contemporary features.

The Traditional Collection offers raised ranches, tudors, split levels, and other traditional houses. Ranging from the 1,102-square-foot Salem, a compact three-bedroom ranch, to the stately Coventry, a 3,820-square-foot tudor with five bedrooms, three and a half baths, and numerous living areas, Northern's Traditional series offers tremendous variety to families seeking new homes.

Northern Homes standard packages

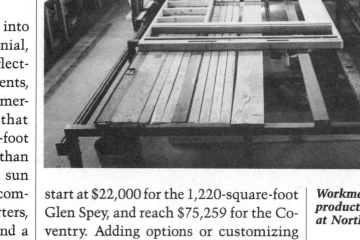

start at $22,000 for the 1,220-square-foot Glen Spey, and reach $75,259 for the Coventry. Adding options or customizing plans increases the purchase price. ∎

Workmen on the production line at Northern Homes.

Each Northern package contains all materials to complete a house shell, including:

- Girders, sill plate, sill insulation, and vapor barrier
- Interior and exterior walls of 2 × 4 or 2 × 6 framing, with waferboard or plywood sheathing
- Exterior 2 × 12 wall headers
- Subfascia, soffit, rafters, and trusses
- Roof sheathing with plywood clips
- Roof shingles
- Floor framing and subflooring
- Siding
- Windows and exterior and interior doors with framing
- Exterior decks
- Interior stairs
- Nails, hardware, and locksets
- Construction plans, construction and detail guide

PACIFIC MODERN HOMES

This home from Pacific Modern offers an attached garage and sloping shed roofs.

Pacific Modern Homes, also known as "Homes by Pacific," has manufactured and packaged home components for over twenty years. In the past, the company has sold packages only to building contractors, but within the last few years it has extended its services to the owner-builder as well. Pacific offers over forty standard plans designed for energy efficiency. The company can package custom-designed homes or modify its standard plans with many custom options.

Pacific markets its homes through a network of dealers in California, Nevada, and Hawaii. These dealers provide advice to customers planning and designing their own homes, and can also recommend reliable builders or furnish assistance to do-it-yourselfers.

Pacific delivers its home kits in two packages—first the exterior, and then the interior materials. When the exterior package arrives, a forklift unloads panels, trusses, and lumber. The wall panels go up with just a crew of four, which can close in a typical Pacific home in a matter of hours. Once they have the trusses in place and the roof sheathing

The Rainier model has a steep-pitched roof and a front balcony.

nailed down, the owners or their subcontractors can add finish roofing and paint the exterior. The entire shell can be finished within a week. Once the interior package arrives, customers are free to complete the interior at their leisure.

A typical home from Pacific, with 1,600 square feet of living area and an attached two-car garage, averages about

$11 per square foot, or $17,600. Pacific also offers barn, garage, and shed packages. ■

The standard exterior package includes:

- 2 × 4 dry Douglas fir interior and exterior panelized walls with siding applied and dual-glazed windows installed
- Exterior embossed metal-insulated doors (including dead-bolt locks), pre-hung
- Dual-glazed sliding glass doors
- Engineered roof trusses
- Roof sheathing
- Nails, metal tieplates, framing clips, Z-bar, step shingles, eaves, gable vents, and caulking
- Exterior trim

The standard interior package contains:

- Kitchen and bathroom cabinets, assembled and pre-finished
- Interior doors, pre-hung, pre-finished, and ready to install, with hardware
- Sliding wardrobe doors, pre-finished and ready to hang
- Closet, linen, and storage shelves
- Medicine cabinets
- Towel bars and tissue holders
- Interior door and baseboard moldings

TOPSIDER HOMES

I can't begin to tell you what a fantastic house this is, in my opinion," says Fred Hall, a Topsider dealer in Union Beach, New Jersey. "It's a unique house. Topsider has been marketing the same design for eighteen years—that'll give you some idea of how well-designed the house is in the first place. It can adapt to any situation—your imagination is the only limit."

Based in Yadkinville, North Carolina, Topsider manufactures and sells eight-sided houses. Some Topsider homes, such as its most popular model, the Treehouse, rest on one-story-high pedestals. The company also makes houses—called "patio homes"—that sit directly on the ground, and offers combination homes which make use of both house types. Developers have used Topsider houses in resort areas including Walt Disney World in Florida, Hilton Head in North Carolina, and Lake of the Ozarks in Arkansas.

"These houses have been primarily marketed as vacation homes up till

Two Topsider pod units are joined on a sloping site for a spacious home with great views.

A two-bedroom plan makes efficient use of space.

now," says Fred, "but I think they make great year-round homes. I just opened my dealership and have sold two homes already. I'm the only Topsider dealer in New Jersey at the present time. People see my model home here in Union Beach and come into the office and say 'What is that thing down the street? I've never seen anything like it.' They want to know how big it is and how much it costs. In fact, most people who come in here want to buy the model home for themselves! I saw these houses in North Carolina during a vacation down there, and was really impressed by them. They are incredibly strong, what I call 'over-designed'—they're stronger than they need to be, floor to ceiling."

"Most of our homes are sold to developers," says Topsider president Sheldon Storer. "We have retail dealerships in some areas, but individual buyers usually deal directly with one of our customer service representatives in North Carolina. These representatives are not commissioned salespeople, but are trained to act as sources of assistance. They can help arrange a visit to the nearest model home, aid in selecting specifications, and generally assist customers in becoming Topsider owners." Topsider dealers throughout the country maintain model homes, and customers can walk through a number of models at the factory in North Carolina. Sales representatives at Topsider's home office not only sell homes, they can provide help in finding builders, securing the necessary building permits, and obtaining financing. In areas served by retail dealerships, dealers perform the same functions. In addition, the company's staff of licensed architects and en-

gineers assist customers in designing their homes, and some dealers provide construction services.

Topsider manufactures roof, wall, and floor panels, and ships them via tractor-trailer to buyers' sites. Most homes require just one 45-foot-long trailer load, but some of the larger models fill more than one truck. At the site, the panels, precision-engineered for a tight fit, bolt together by means of pre-drilled holes. Exterior wall sections, doors, windows, and sliding glass doors fasten to the structural members as in conventional construction. Once they've built their shell, customers can finish the interior of their home using locally available materials. Topsider can also supply prefabricated interiors for certain models.

"Any licensed contractor should easily

Top: A greenhouse passage connects two standard units.

Bottom: A Topsider home fits well on a woodland site.

be able to build your home in about thirty days' time, using only a small crew," says Sheldon Storer. "In fact, most contractors find our homes easier, faster, and more efficient to build than homes employing conventional construction techniques." To aid customers in obtaining contractors' bids, Topsider supplies a full set of architectural drawings and a step-by-step building manual giving the details of assembly, as well as a half-hour-long videotape presentation that shows the construction process, from foundation excavation to kit completion.

An advantage of the Topsider construction method is that it allows many customers to build their homes themselves or serve as their own general contractors if they choose. "We recommend that people considering building their homes themselves be reasonably familiar with carpentry tools and have some construction skills," says Sheldon Storer. "It's not really a house for a complete amateur. In addition, we recommend that the mechanical details, such as the masonry work, wiring, and plumbing, be subcontracted."

Topsider offers versatility in design as well as in construction. "These houses can adapt to any site, any situation," says Fred Hall. "They can be very grand or very simple. One house I'm building now has private maid's quarters. I'm planning on building a development of freestanding townhouses here in Union Beach, and as single units they make large, attractive private homes. They're good also as time-share units and vacation homes. They can be as big or as small as you want them to be. I'm planning to build a two-story residence for my wife and me, with an elevator since she's not so good at getting around. They really are extremely flexible."

The company manufactures nine different standard models, including two structures intended as garages. Standard models range in size from 475 square feet to 1,500 square feet, and come in pedestal or patio versions, with one or two stories.

Topsider's original and most popular model, the Treehouse, ranges from 900 to 1,000 square feet in size and sits atop a pedestal. It offers complete freedom in

A single story patio model sits directly on the ground.

Lots of glass gives access to good views.

interior design because none of the interior walls are loadbearing. The Campsider represents a patio version of the Treehouse. Particulary well suited to level building sites, this single-story home sits directly on the ground. Both the Campsider and its companion building, the 108 Garage, measure 800 square feet in area.

The Slopesider, a two-story version of the Treehouse, includes the pedestal feature, as well as a spiral staircase and wedge-shaped ground floor enclosures. Intended for sloping sites, this model makes use of up to five such enclosures, yielding floorspace of a maximum of 1,500 square feet — Topsider's largest single-unit home.

Topsider designed another pedestal model, the Skisider, especially for small, difficult sites, and also manufactures a patio version, which it calls the Trailsider. Both run about 575 square feet in area, and the Trailsider can also serve as a garage. Two-story models include the Treetopper, a single- or multi-family unit designed for on-grade construction; and the Treesider, a smaller version of the Treetopper.

For customers who want larger homes, Topsider offers combinations of standard units. The company can supply, on request, drawings of a variety of such configurations. Many customers who build Topsiders as their primary residences build a number of standard units and attach them to form larger houses. The company provides design assistance for those who choose to do so.

Every Topsider home offers interior design flexibility. Because the exterior

Many customers build a number of standard units and attach them to form larger houses.

walls bear the weight of the roof, the doors, windows, and interior partitions can go almost anywhere. Customers can mix and match most standard interior layouts with most Topsider models. The

Topsider homes adapt to many different sites.

company has a portfolio of suggested floorplans to help buyers make their design decisions. These designs generally include one or two bedrooms, a living/dining area, kitchen, and bath, and most make especially good vacation homes. For some of its models, Topsider can furnish plans which adapt the houses for use as multi-family duplex or fourplex units.

Topsider sells many options as upgrades to its standard plans. Its panelized interior for single-story models features paneling and trim of finished premium-grade Southern Yellow Pine. The pre-wired interior includes two bedrooms, storage closets, two pre-plumbed fiberglas bathroom modules, a living area, dining area, and a complete kitchen with pre-finished cabinets, a double-basin stainless steel sink, and an eating bar.

Extended floor trusses, spiral staircases, and exterior decks can add variety to standard designs. Topsider decks come in a range of depths, from 4½ feet

to 9½ feet. Each extends the length of one of the house's eight sides, so that eight would make a wraparound deck. Two extended floor trusses, available in a variety of styles, support each deck section.

Windows and doors come in a choice of clear, tinted, or reflective double-glazed glass, and corner windows offer the further option of triple-glazed obscure glass. Customers can choose either fixed or openable windows. Doors come in a variety of styles, including ja-

Owners can design their own interiors.

130

lousie models with wood slats, sliding glass models, wood styles with glass panels, and solid metal doors. Wall frames that replace entire wall panels with three bay sliding glass doors or other door/window combinations round off the list of window and door options.

Topsider customers can choose from a variety of panel insulation packages. Standard floor and roof panels come with six inches of fiberglass batt insulation and offer an insulating value of R-22. For an additional $2,399, five and a half inches of rigid foam board in the panels brings the R-value up to 40. Three inches of fiberglass supply Topsider's standard walls with an R-value of 11, but with the addition of rigid foam for $100 per panel, the walls can provide an insulating value of up to R-19.

The company's optional high wind load and seismic package incorporates special steel rods and plates into the solid wall panels. This option ensures that houses meet Seismic IV stability requirements and can withstand winds of up to 140 miles per hour. Another Topsider modification that provides added protection from the elements is the extended roof soffit overhang, which adds an extra foot to the soffit.

Prices for basic Topsider kits range from $9,990 for a garage to $31,990 for a 1,500-square-foot Treetopper, the largest model manufactured by Topsider. The Treehouse — Topsider's most popular model — costs $25,990 for the standard model. Options add to the total cost of a house: The panelized interior costs $6,990; deck sections cost between $500 and $650 each, with supporting trusses an additional $200 to $300 each; and extra insulation can add even more. ∎

Units used in combination allow a variety of designs, in addition to more living space.

A basic Topsider shell package contains the following materials:

- All structural members except foundation materials (available as options)
- Eight insulated roof panels
- Roofing felt
- Roof truss
- Wall frames as necessary
- Windows and doors as per design
- Corner panels as per design
- Eight insulated floor panels for pedestal and two-story models (not required for patio models)
- Floor trusses
- Basement pedestal closure materials

Topsider offers the following as options:

- Deck packages: pre-cut decking, perlins, joists, facias, handrails, pre-drilled pickets, all hardware and fasteners
- Galvanized steel frame and treated lumber packages
- Extended roof soffit overhang
- Spiral staircase of welded steel, with handrails, posts, and treads
- Appliances, carpet, window blinds, furniture, fireplaces, miscellaneous building supplies and materials

LOG AND TIMBER WALL HOMES

*F*or those who love the solid, rustic aspect of a log home but thought they could never build one, kit homes provide a practical alternative. Log homes have come a long way from their humble beginnings as makeshift pioneer shelters with dirt floors and few, if any, windows. Now they often incorporate such features as exposed timber trusses, soaring cathedral ceilings, floor-to-ceiling glass windows, Jacuzzis, hot tubs, and greenhouses.

Log homes, and timber wall homes in general, have certain advantages over other types of construction, especially for do-it-yourselfers. The walls and roof go up relatively quickly and remain nearly maintenance-free. Log homes don't require costly insulation, since the logs themselves insulate the interior of the house and create a thermal storage mass that absorbs the heat of the sun. The logs in a kit home arrive cut and ready to assemble, requiring only the use of ordinary carpenter's tools. And during the cold months, builders find it easier to construct log homes than other types of structures. They close the shell with hammers and

spikes and then work in the heated interior to finish the home.

Log homes need the same kind of site preparation as regular homes, and offer the same choice of foundations, from full basements to post and pier arrangements. Builders should finish the foundation and subflooring before the logs arrive so they won't have to store them on the ground too long. They

should cover the logs to prevent ice damage if a construction delay requires storage in cold weather.

Log homes lend themselves to flexible interior designs. The load-bearing logs allow builders to place interior partitions anywhere, usually employing conventional stud construction. Some manufacturers offer paneling to those desiring the look of a complete wood interior. Log kits, however, generally do not include any materials beyond the log shell itself, making it necessary either to purchase flooring, paneling, roofing, etc., from the manufacturer as an option or buy it locally.

Placement of plumbing lines and electrical wiring requires extra care. Many manufacturers design kits with recesses in the base log to hold wiring

or else run it around windows or door frames and conceal it with trim. Homeowners can easily hide plumbing lines in the interior partition wall that usually encloses the bathroom.

All logs require treatment with sealers or preservatives to protect against insect infestation and rot. Most manufacturers dip their logs in a solution approved by the Environmental Protection Agency. The longer the logs soak, the better the protection. Several log home manufacturers provide a warranty against infestation and rot for several years. While some companies offer untreated logs as an option, a few others sell only this kind, believing that preservatives detract from the wood's beauty, and that the periodic application of clear sealer provides ample maintenance.

Log home manufacturers supply different shapes and sizes of logs for their home kits, including:

- □ Logs flattened top and bottom, with rounded sides
- □ Three-sided logs, with flat inner face and rounded exterior
- □ Logs with four flat faces
- □ Hand-peeled logs with bits of bark remaining for a more rustic look
- □ Machine-peeled logs for a smooth look

The various types of lumber for log buildings include: white northern cedar, white and red pine, spruce, yellow poplar, and jackpine.

Because of their popularity, long delays in the delivery of log kits can occur, especially during the busy season—late spring, summer, and early fall. ■

APPALACHIAN LOG STRUCTURES

"I decided to build a log home for three reasons," says Albert Bretz of Galloway, Ohio, who bought a kit from Appalachian. "First of all, the excellent construction. A log home is extremely well-built. It's really a solid structure. Second, it's relatively easy to build one. It's a lot of hard work, but everything falls into place and there's no cutting to do. Third, these structures have terrific longevity. This home was really the best-built, the most 'high tech' log home on the market."

Appalachian Log Structures offers a variety of buildings, from two-car attached garages to multi-unit townhouses and condominium complexes. Based in Ripley, West Virginia, the company sells forty standard models, including single- and two-story homes, commercial structures, and vacation homes. Appalachian can engineer a house to meet building codes anywhere in the country.

The company even offers a variety of log types. Its most popular type, pressure-treated pine, the strongest softwood available, features a straight grain that lends dimensional stability. Other

A log home can offer plenty of room for relaxed family living.

The Travis model provides 1,343 square feet of living space including three bedrooms.

options, such as oak, walnut, and cherry, create a log home that has the feel of crafted furniture.

Pressure-treating pine with CCA (chromated-copper-arsenate metal salts) produces logs with a clean, odor-free, earth-tone finish that requires no further treatment with stain or paint. The solution penetrates the cellular structure of the wood, forming a chemical bond that shields against rot and insect infestation. The company backs up its treatment

> *"I like my home for its rustic look," says a recent customer. "It's real old-timey and has great warmth and atmosphere."*

process with a twenty-five-year warranty against insect damage and decay, in addition to the two-year warranty that covers cut and fit. The finished logs are non-toxic, but if you prefer, you can order untreated packages from the company. These, however, do not come with the additional twenty-five-year warranty.

Appalachian buyers also have a choice of log styles, which come in 6- or 8-inch thick sizes. The traditional Appalachian Round has a rounded exterior face, while the Shadolog has more of a contemporary look. The flattened and machine-beveled surface of the Shadolog gives the

appearance of classical horizontal clapboard siding even as it maintains the benefits of log construction.

A home built in the energy-efficient Mountaineer Dovetail style has alternating layers of 10-inch high logs and chink-joint spacer logs to produce a more airtight wall. Appalachian bevels the chink-joint log on the outside to shed water. A recess allows the easy application of chinking for aesthetic purposes. The wall requires no additional sealing.

Traditional log beams supply a warm ambience.

135

"I like my new home, which is a Mountaineer Dovetail, for its rustic look," says Lois Rice of Jefferson, Ohio, who first built a small two-bedroom ranch with her husband and then became an enthusiastic dealer for the company. "It's real old-timey and has a great warmth and atmosphere."

All three log styles have a flattened, V-jointed interior face, which makes finishing work, such as framing partitions, applying trim, and installing cabinets, much easier. Buyers can apply paneling and wallboard directly over the log surface.

Appalachian offers a choice of foundations, including pressure-treated posts and all-weather wood foundations. Purchasers can also install a crawl space or have a masonry contractor build a conventional concrete block foundation for a full basement.

Albert Bretz designed his own home, as do about 90 percent of the people who choose Appalachian. He decided what he wanted in the house, and the company drew up the plans with a few minor modifications. "The changes that they made resulted in a house that we liked even better than our original design, so we sent those plans back and told them to go ahead with the final plans."

Standard components of an Appalachian kit include all log walls, plus windows and doors.

Appalachian doesn't charge for its design service. Prospective homeowners can modify any of the standard plans to get what they want, according to Lois Rice. She and her husband have just built a new house with 1,400 square feet, including an upstairs loft. "People come in to look at our model home," she says, "and they want to know how the houses are put together, how they can build one themselves, how much it will cost. I tell them you can get a design from anywhere—a magazine, a plan book, even from another company—or, of course, from Appalachian—and send it in with your specifications and modifications."

Lois has sold homes to many couples

The Spencer offers exposed-beam ceilings and three bedrooms.

Pre-cut mortise and tenon joints create secure corner seals.

where one partner was at first considerably less enthusiastic than the other. "Some people think a log home is still something from Abe Lincoln's day—with dirt floors. They're surprised at the level of comfort available. These are really very sophisticated homes. Buying a log house doesn't mean going back to the olden days."

Appalachian's design department can turn even the roughest sketches into blueprints. Starting with a customer's basic design concept, the company works out a tentative quote. The customer decides whether to proceed or to make further modifications. Once they know the budget for a particular house, the company designers draw up floor plans. After the customer approves the plans, the designers produce blueprints based on the owner's choice of foundation, construction materials, location of the foundation on the site, type of windows, style and pitch of the roof, size of porches or decks, and other design features.

Appalachian Round-style logs are rounded on the outside for a traditional look, and flat on the inside.

The blueprints provide two exterior elevations (renderings of various façades of the house), foundation dimensions, framing details, a cross section view, and a set of standard construction specs common to most Appalachian structures.

An Appalachian log kit includes pre-cut and numbered logs and a clearly written construction manual, simplifying the building process, especially for the novice. The manual describes the tools and materials used to construct the house. The do-it-yourselfer can use the manual to plan a budget; the professional contractor, to prepare a cost estimate.

"Most people do their own building to save money," says Lois. "Some people might have friends come in and help them with the framing, and have a subcontractor do the interior finishing, the plumbing, the wiring, and so on. The average person will attempt a log home because it seems less complicated, and it really is. Appalachian supplies technical assistance if required. If you keep the logs in order, you won't have any problems."

"This house went together very well — I had very little trouble," says Albert Bretz of the home he built. "Appalachian has a reputation for easy assembly, and I checked with other owner-builders to confirm it before I started." He hired a subcontractor to build only the foundation. Working mostly on weekends with a crew of friends who helped him, Albert raised the shell in two months, a period which included some weather delays. "It wasn't difficult," he says, "although it's not a job for a lazy person. It helps to have ambition and some help, which I did.

Left: Most home-owners find it easy to build their Appalachian kits themselves.

Opposite page: Exposed beams and stone fireplaces make for a country-style interior. Below: Dormer windows add light and space to lofts.

Taking your time, not hurrying—you just keep on adding those logs to the wall, one on top of the other. I did have one setback. It rained three weekends out of one month. Eighteen days of rain! I sat with my buddies each day out at the site, drinking coffee under the shelter of the tarp, hoping it would stop. With this delay, I didn't get to put the windows in until December. There I was, hanging them from the outside on the second story, thirty feet up, while it was eight degrees below.

"But not all of it was like that. Building the house was fun most of the time, or I wouldn't have done it. We have an album of snapshots, and we took videotapes of the construction. It's lots of fun to look back on. I even did my own drywall partitions. I truly believe that I have the best-constructed log home in the industry. You don't need any machinery to build the house—you can do it all yourself."

Appalachian offers numerous special features to make construction and maintenance of its log structures easier. For example, window and jamb slots allow doors and windows to continue to fit smoothly even when the logs settle. Adjustable steel anchors run through the wall from top to bottom, binding logs together at corners, windows, and door openings and eliminating warping. As logs shrink and shift, which they tend to do in any of these houses, adjusting the

The Farm House design offers a living/dining room with a beamed cathedral ceiling.

wall anchors pulls them more tightly together.

"You just go down into the basement and tighten the wall anchors every six months or so," says Albert. "It's really a great idea—as the house settles, it became tighter and tighter."

Prices of Appalachian log structures vary according to the log style chosen, with models featuring the Mountaineer Dovetail wall costing the most. The modified Spencer model, which Lois built, costs $16,500 for the Mountaineer Dovetail package, and $15,000 for either Shadolog or Appalachian Round. The price goes up with the addition of optional items, such as a post foundation, subfloor, or special roof kit, which can add several thousand dollars to the cost of a basic package. ■

A standard kit from Appalachian includes:

- All logs, pressure-treated and pre-cut to size, with milled tongue and groove notched ends, ship-lap joints, pre-drilled holes for spikes, and openings for windows and doors
- All structural lumber: pre-cut rafters, collar ties, support posts, ridge beams, jambs, sill, sill returns, plates, porch posts, in addition to joists and girder beams for lofts and two-story homes
- All wood trim: facing boards, window and door facings, baseboards, gable end sliding, and tongue and groove siding to cover subfloor perimeter beam
- Anderesen Permashield Narroline thermopane windows
- Pre-hung wooden exterior doors
- All anchors, spikes, sealant, beam hangers, lag screws, settlement adjusters
- Construction guide
- Three sets of blueprints

Optional packages include:

- Foundation systems, either all-weather wood foam-core panels or pressure-treated wood posts
- Subfloor packages
- Roof packages, including pressure-treated roof shakes and foam-core insulated roofing panels
- Porches, lofts, and dormers
- Gable ends of pre-cut, pressure-treated logs
- Lower-cost windows
- Kiln drying

The homeowner must supply studding for interior partitions, a truss rafter system, finish flooring, electrical wiring, plumbing, heating system, fixtures, closets, stairways, and kitchen cabinets.

The smooth inner surfaces of all three Appalachian log styles create the look of wood paneling.

Traditional decorative touches harmonize with the log interior.

BEAVER LOG HOMES

The Broken Arrow features a covered porch and a stone fireplace.

Beaver Log Homes offers pre-cut log kits that customers can either build themselves or have built by a contractor. The company uses a variety of pine and other wood species, and the logs are machine-peeled and turned from whole trees to a uniform diameter of 8, 10, or 12 inches. Once peeled and turned, logs are milled with a double tongue and groove top and bottom.

In addition to the double tongue and groove system, the company uses saddle-notched corners, with half-circles milled into the bottoms of corner logs. These notches serve to interlock the wall courses, strengthening the walls and speeding construction. As the wall is built, a specially designed saddle gasket goes between the logs as a sealant.

Beaver homes can be erected on virtually any conventional foundation system, including a full basement. Some models feature interior log walls that serve to separate the living area from an

The 512-square-foot Trapper makes a good vacation cabin.

142

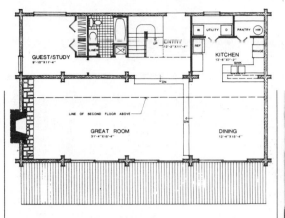

attached garage, and to provide roof support. Otherwise, most homes incorporate interior partitions of the conventional stud frame variety.

The wiring and plumbing installation is easy. Both systems go in the same way they would in a frame building. Outlets and switches can also be installed in exterior walls by morticing the logs and running the wires through channels bored or chiseled at the appropriate points.

Six mills located throughout the country—in Colorado, Wisconsin, Michigan, Texas, and Missouri—produce Beaver

homes. Dealers set their own prices: the company doesn't provide a standard price list. To get the number of the dealer nearest you, call the Beaver home office in Nebraska.

Beaver materials packages include only the logs, plus optional sealing materials. The company's experience has convinced it that customers can buy items such as windows, doors, beams, and trusses much less expensively from local sources. ■

Top, left: The Cascade offers three bedrooms and a contemporary exterior.

Top, right: Beaver homes offer comfortable rustic living.

Middle & bottom: Exposed beams and log walls make for old-fashioned interiors.

143

CEDAR FOREST PRODUCTS

Cedar Forest Products manufactures laminated, pre-cut cedar timber wall homes. CFP offers many different standard home designs that can be modified to personal tastes. The company even gives customers a choice of corner styles—rustic "log cabin" ends or "Salem square." Either style provides complete protection against wind and weather.

To ensure strength, CFP makes its walls of five-part bonded laminate. The end-matched timbers meet precisely when assembled, and dovetail corners provide a reliable weather seal. After the timbers are pre-cut at the plant, workers pre-assemble each house to make sure all the components fit perfectly. After that, they dismantle the house and ship it to the building site.

Laminated beams of Western red cedar use tongue and groove joints for tight, well-constructed walls.

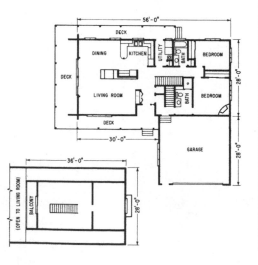

The Bartlett model from Cedar Forest Products offer 1,500 square feet of living space on two floors.

Each CFP shell package comes with:

- All exterior wall timbers, 5 × 8 Western red cedar, pre-cut and routed or drilled for wiring
- Assembled roof trusses
- Assembled gable ends, covered with tongue and groove red cedar paneling
- Roof system of plywood sheathing, felting, and fiberglass shingles
- Plywood cornice with cedar fascia
- Solid core mahogany exterior doors
- Double-hung wood-framed insulated windows with screens
- All exterior trim
- Rough and finish hardware
- Second floor system

A complete kit includes all of the above plus:

- Hollow core mahogany interior doors
- 2 × 4 interior partitions with Sheetrock
- Sheetrock ceilings with fiberglass insulation
- Cedar interior trim

Preassembled roof trusses and gable ends create architectural drama.

A prow-front chalet design incorporates a wraparound deck.

Pre-drilled holes for nails speed construction of CFP homes. Depending on the complexity of their plans, owners can either build their home themselves or hire professional help. CFP can provide supervision or complete contracting services.

CFP offers shell packages, complete kits, and special kits for homes with cathedral ceilings (because they require different finishing), as well as separate floor system kits. House prices start at $13,970 for a 528-square-foot shell package, and go up to $53,222 for a 2,688-square-foot complete package with attached garage. ∎

GASTINEAU LOG HOMES

Among U.S. kit home companies, according to Gastineau, only it offers log homes in three woods: oak, pine, and walnut. Almost 90 percent of its customers choose the air-dried Missouri white and red oak logs. The company doesn't treat any of its logs with preservatives, believing that builders should only spray the exterior of the constructed house to leave interior surfaces free of the odor and unnatural coloring these chemicals sometimes add. With a standard diameter of 7½ inches, the logs arrive in random lengths of 8 to 16 feet, allowing for last-minute changes from the plans.

Gastineau homes range in size from small cabins to spacious four-bedroom homes. With 1,440 square feet, the Bonanza features fireplaces in both the living room and master bedroom, plus two additional bedrooms, two baths, a dining room, kitchen, and even a utility room and front porch. The loft option offers an additional 920 square feet of space and two gable ends on the exterior. The smaller Aspen model has two upstairs bedrooms, a cathedral ceiling in the liv-

This expanded version of the Bricketwood features a tudor-style second floor exterior.

The Osage offers three bedrooms in 2,490 square feet of living space.

ing room, 1½ baths, a fireplace, kitchen, dining area, and a 13 × 19-foot living room. The building has outside dimensions of 40 × 32 feet.

The one-floor Terra-Firma provides an unusual approach to energy-efficient construction. In this "earth contact" design, the back and end walls remain below ground, and large windows on the front log wall provide ample light. The 2,140-square-foot home provides three bedrooms, a cathedral ceiling in the living room and in the large solarium, a large pantry in the kitchen, and a central fireplace. Gastineau's designers can also customize other models to employ the earth-contact system.

For oak or southern yellow pine double tongue and groove logs, prices for full kits with basements range from $16,675 for the 840-square-foot Grizzly Adams to $45,275 for the 3,128-square-foot Pasadena. The Bonanza with the loft option carries a price of $32,775; the Aspen, $29,950. The Terra-Firma, available only on a slab foundation, costs $32,450. Buyers can order full kits for most models or just the shells, and have the option of a basement or slab foundation. Gastineau also offers a "Lay-Away/Save-A-Way" plan that allows home builders to buy logs at the current price for a home to be built up to thirty months later. ■

A standard full kit contains:

- ☐ **All logs specified in the design**
- ☐ **Subflooring for first and second floors, with joists, girders, etc.**
- ☐ **Interior wall studs and plates**
- ☐ **All steps**
- ☐ **Roofing, trusses, or rafters as required**
- ☐ **Gable end siding as specified; vents, soffit, etc. as required**
- ☐ **Exterior and interior doors, pre-hung**
- ☐ **Wood thermal-paned pre-hung windows**
- ☐ **Nails**
- ☐ **Sealer for log walls**
- ☐ **Blueprints. Major changes to standard plans cost extra.**

Optional materials include pine ceiling or wall decking, shake wood shingles, major appliances, and cabinets.

Top & middle: Gastineau interiors can have a contemporary or traditional style.

Left: The Summerset has covered porches in front and back.

GREATWOOD LOG HOMES

The Montana model offers a great room with a cathedral ceiling.

Mary Hertel owns a Greatwood log home in Oostburg, Wisconsin, which her family uses as a weekend retreat. They had always wanted a log cabin, and the design fit in with the rustic atmosphere on their wooded property. "We chose Greatwood," Mary says, "because we checked around and felt that we'd be happiest with a Greatwood product. They hand-peel all the logs at the site, so every log has a unique shape and texture. It's not like a house with machine-peeled logs, where you have a wall of twenty logs that are exactly alike.

"I did a lot of research before I chose which house to build," says Jane Shore, another Greatwood homeowner. "I looked at log homes as just one possibility, and then we decided that a log home would be most appropriate to the site, and most suitable in terms of our budget and land. It's also in keeping with the rural area where the house is located."

Greatwood Log Homes, based in Elkhart Lake, Wisconsin, manufactures its logs from handcrafted Northern white cedar, which resists checking and cracking, requires little upkeep, and lasts a long time. The company also offers less expensive pine logs.

Customers can construct a Greatwood Full Log home on any type of foundation, from a full basement to a crawl space. Homeowners choose interior partitions of either conventional lumber with optional paneling, or full log construction, which costs more. The company mills the interior surfaces of the logs flat to a uniform height of about 5 inches, and its workers add V-notched corners. They nail in 10-inch spikes at 2-foot intervals, and place ¾-inch diameter steel rods running vertically at corners, windows, and door openings, to create a secure wall. Two strips of insulation between each log and interior and exterior caulking make the wall airtight.

Unlike Full Log homes, Ultra Log homes have logs milled flat on three sides and well-insulated on the interior wall surface. With 15-lb. felt and 1-inch styrofoam sheathing on 2 × 6 studs, and 6 inches of fiberglass in the wall cavity, Ultra Logs have R-values of up to R-30, and Ultra Log roofs of R-40. From the outside, the Ultra Log wall looks like a traditional Full Log wall, but the interior offers a choice of finishes, from full log siding or knotty pine paneling to drywall.

Greatwood's custom design service offers free modification of any plans adapted from its gallery of standard designs. The company's design staff can also turn the customer's own ideas into custom plans.

"I designed our log home myself," says Jane Shore. "I didn't pick it out of a magazine or take it from a plan book. I drew the floor plan, which had some similarities to one of Greatwood's stock plans, and then played around with it and got it to work the way I wanted it to. I sent it in to Greatwood, and they agreed that they could build it. They didn't charge me any kind of design fee. The staff designer looked at the plan and made a few changes. He added skylights where he thought it would be too dark without them. He was right. He also helped me to resolve the problems I was having in working out a screened-in porch to go with the roofline. That was a big help, because it really kind of had me stumped."

Now, she says, "I love everything about this house. It has full logs inside and out, so it has a rustic quality that is also low-maintenance."

For their small house near Lake Michigan, the Hertels took the basic plan from the Greatwood plan book and "then fiddled with it a little," according to Mary. The cabin has a front porch and a back screened porch, a great room with a cathedral ceiling, two bedrooms on the first floor, and a loft space above. "Most

Beamed ceilings and a window wall are features of the Montana.

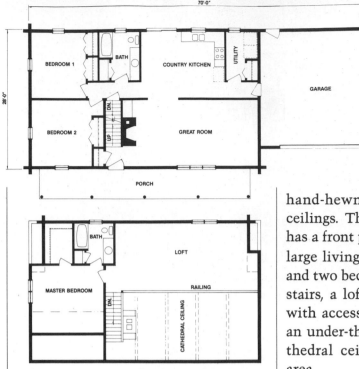

of the time we use just the fireplace to heat the house," notes Mary. "But sometimes when it's really cold, we use the electric baseboard heat. Sometimes we'll come to stay for the weekend and the house will be at 40 degrees, so we just light the fire in the fireplace and turn on the electric heat to warm it up. And that's the last time we use the electric heat all weekend."

Greatwood offers complete construction services for its log homes, or customers can do some of the work themselves. "We had Greatwood contract it out for us," says Jane. "We live sixty miles from the site and couldn't really supervise. Besides, I think it's important to use local craftspeople on a project. They have pride in what they do for the community and they're right there if something goes wrong. They don't have to make a 120-mile roundtrip in order to fix it. The house was under construction from November to the following June. It took longer to build than we expected because we had a terrible winter and there was a lot of snow, so the construction crew couldn't work every day. In addition, hand-peeling the logs is something of a time-consuming process."

Greatwood offers a variety of designs in its stock home portfolio. Many feature hand-hewn log trusses and cathedral ceilings. The Elkhart, a typical model, has a front porch and a back deck, and a large living room, dining area, kitchen, and two bedrooms on the first floor. Upstairs, a loft contains a third bedroom, with access to an outdoor balcony and an under-the-eaves storage space. A cathedral ceiling rises above the living area.

The Shoreview, with nearly 2,400 square feet, represents one of the larger home designs from Greatwood. The first-floor plan includes a great room with a cathedral ceiling, two bedrooms, a bath, and a utility room. The great room connects to both a wraparound exterior deck and a screened-in porch. Upstairs, a loft looks out over the great room. This level also contains a closet storage area, three-quarter bath, master bedroom, and outside balcony across the back of the house.

In addition to its series of traditional models, Greatwood also offers a passive

Top: This three bedroom model offers extra privacy for the master bedroom.

The Ellison model has a master bedroom suite with a balcony.

Beamed cathedral ceilings, in combination with hand-peeled logs, create an elegant but rustic interior.

solar homes group. These designs include both direct gain and isolated gain solar systems.

Greatwood also has a third method of protecting a home against extremes of temperature, called the "solar envelope." This method works by super-insulating the house and creating a flow of air around the living space. These houses, constructed with a double north wall, have 12 inches of air space—called a plenum—between the inner and outer walls. The house also has a roof plenum. These plena interconnect with each other and with another in the basement. The south wall contains a solarium space with a wood deck floor. Cool air from the basement chamber rises into the solarium, heating up and then flowing through the ceiling plenum and the north wall back into the basement. During the summer, a geothermal cooling tube removes moisture from the outside air through condensation, and cools the air to 50-55 degrees. The system draws cool air up into the solarium and vents hot air with an attic fan.

Prices for Greatwood log homes vary according to the materials and features selected. The Ultra-Log insulated wall costs less than the Full Log wall, but the higher R-value option adds to the price.

Greatwood's smallest log home, the 320-square-foot Hudson, costs $9,900 for the Ultra Log in pine, $13,545 for the cedar Ultra-Log, $14,595 for Full Log pine, and $15,957 for Full Log cedar. An outdoor porch adds $390 to the total. A larger home, such as the nearly 2,400-square-foot Shoreview, costs from $47,713 to $53,484. An outdoor deck or porch adds nearly $3,000 to the price of the home. ∎

A standard package of a Greatwood Full Log home includes:

- Exterior Full Log wall system, with V-notched mitered corners
- Thermopane double-hung wood windows, aluminum-clad, with combination storm/screens and removable grills
- Solid wood exterior doors and storm/screen doors
- 10-inch steel spikes
- ¾-inch steel rods
- Window and door insulating splines
- Ultra-Seal gasket stripping for exterior walls
- Wood-tone caulk
- Second floor stairs and floor system
- 2 × 2 roof framing or trusses
- Roof sheathing
- 9-inch fiberglass batt insulation
- Fiberglass roof shingles
- Knotty-pine soffits and cedar fascia
- Vapor barrier
- Continuous ridge and soffit vents
- Metal valley flashing
- Log rafters, tie beams, posts and diagonal members, and beam hardware for cathedral ceiling
- 2 × 4 and 2 × 6 studs, and 2-inch nominal door headers for interior walls

HERITAGE LOG HOMES

Almost half of Heritage's new customers come through referrals from the owners of the company's log homes. The company delivers either a basic shell or a dry-in shell, which includes a roof system. It offers about forty models, ranging from small cabins to rambling homes perfect for large families. In addition to selling standard models, the company will modify its designs to taste or design custom homes. Heritage offers a thirty year limited warranty on its kits.

Heritage uses fully milled, seasoned yellow pine for its logs, with a double tongue and groove system to create a snug fit between them. The specially designed jamb for windows and doors helps to maintain the lateral strength of the walls while decreasing possible air leakage. The company offers several other design features to boost energy efficiency. In its passive solar homes, for example, a ventilation duct system pumps hot air outside in the summer and recycles it inside during the winter months.

With five bedrooms, three and one-half baths, a family room, and cathedral ceilings in both the living room and country kitchen, the Waterville model supplies a roomy 3,692 square feet of

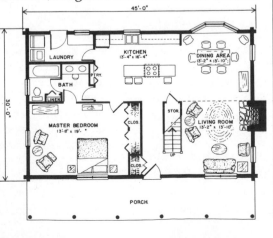

*The four-bedroom
Cedaridge has a
bay window in the
dining room and
a cathedral ceiling
in the living room.*

A basic shell includes:

- Full log exterior walls
- Solid wood windows and exterior doors
- Machine-surfaced beams, timbers, joists, rafters, etc.
- All sealant materials
- 10-inch spikes
- Three or more blueprints and log placement drawings
- Construction manual
- On-site assistance

The Dry-in Shell also includes:

- 4 × 8-foot insulated roof panels (available with R-20 or R-30 ratings)
- Tar paper
- Roofing nails

Heritage ships from four locations to all states and Canada.

Top three: Many Heritage owners favor traditional interior design features.

living space. Other features include a separate laundry room, back porch, workbench area, attached garage, and generous closets and storage areas. Another model, the Elkmont, features a loft, three bedrooms, a fireplace, and a 13 × 20-foot living room for a total living area of 1,636 square feet. The home only occupies 30 × 35 feet, which makes it suitable for smaller building sites. The Waterville's basic shell costs $39,900; the dry-in shell, $52,200 with a standard roof system. A super-insulation package runs an additional $5,600, while tongue and groove decking for the second floor costs another $2,100. The Elkmont has a price of $17,500 for the basic shell and $20,600 for the dry-in shell and standard roof system. Heritage estimates that a finished home typically costs three to four times the basic shell price. Owner-builders can reduce this figure, while putting in special features increases it. ∎

Bottom: Customers can purchase houses or garages with gambrel roofs.

INTERNATIONAL HOMES OF CEDAR

Everybody knows about ordinary homes, but nobody is familiar with the kind of houses I build," says Robin Loughran, owner of Cedar Dreams, an International Cedar Homes dealership serving New Jersey and eastern Pennsylvania. "When I show people my houses, they think they're really something special, and they're surprised they didn't know about them before. I have to educate my clients as to what to expect, explain to them what a laminated cedar wall home is. It's not a log cabin, it's not like a kitchen countertop—it's a beautiful, unusual wood house, warm in the winter, cool in the summer, well-insulated, and easy to maintain—a special house."

For people interested in a wood home, especially those who want something a little bit out of the ordinary, an IHC house may fit the bill. It did for Tim Kiriposki, an IHC owner in Coopersburg, Pennsylvania. "We had been thinking about building a cedar home for twenty years," says Tim. "Then we saw this one at a home show and decided to go ahead with it. It's an A-frame house. The downstairs is open-plan—all one big room, with a balcony overlooking it on three sides upstairs. I like the house because it's all wood all over. The walls, floors, and ceilings are all wood, all the way through. There's only about two pieces of Sheetrock in the whole house, and I love the way it looks."

This member of the Fond Memory Series has 1,500 square feet of living space plus an attached garage.

The first-floor plan of the Timberline model from the Alpine Series.

IHC, based in Woodinville, Washington, offers a unique product: laminated cedar timber wall homes, distinguished by structural strength and ease of construction. The laminated cedar timbers are laid one atop the other to form the exterior wall—a construction method similar to that used in building a log home. The patented interlocking T-joint system ensures that the timbers fit together snugly, and a special adhesive seals each joint, creating a wall resistant to damage from high winds and earthquakes—a wall engineered to last.

The lamination process itself gives birth to IHC's innovative interlocking wall system. For both the standard wall timber—made from three layers of pine or cedar—and the deluxe five-layer timber, IHC positions the boards so that the ends form a rough T-joint. These rough joints are then precision-machined in the factory to fit tightly into one another. This tight bonding ensures a high level of thermal efficiency in the house—little air can infiltrate or escape through the joints.

In addition to its standard wall of 4 × 8 timbers and its deluxe wall of 5 × 8 timbers, IHC offers Thermo-Lam walls, which feature 6 × 8 wall timbers with a core of 1½-inch rigid polyurethane or polystyrene foam insulation. The Thermo-Lam wall acts both as an insulator and as an energy conservation system by combining the natural heat-retaining qualities of wood with the benefits of synthetic insulation. When incorporated into a passive solar system, Thermo-Lam walls function both as a thermal barrier and as a built-in heat-retaining mass.

Tim Kiriposki appreciates the house's energy-efficient nature. "I spent two hundred and fifty dollars last year to heat the house the whole winter—and that's all. The whole thing stays warm with just a seventy-nine-dollar kerosene heater. Now, I know that many people will tell you that's not the best way to do it, but it works for us. I come right inside during the wintertime, put the heater on, and the place heats right up."

IHC's construction system offers kit buyers the benefits of saving both time and money. The house can be owner-built or contracted. Lise Larsen and her husband Benny have built two IHC homes: one is their primary home in Grass Valley, California; the other, a vacation home in the mountains near Lake Tahoe, Nevada. "We made our dream

Wood paneling makes for a casual atmosphere.

house, and we did all the work ourselves. It's fun. It's not really easy, but it's not hard, either—not so hard as to be impossible. My husband had never built anything before he built our mountain house in Tahoe, and that went fine. Building an IHC house is a neat way of building your own home. We love the warmth of wood inside and out, and we find that the house is beautifully insulated and crafted."

"It's easy to put up," says Tim Kiriposki. "Getting the shell up took only four days. It's a very straightforward building system. In fact, my son did most of the work, and he was still in his teens at the time."

"The construction process is completely simple and straightforward," says Robin Loughran. "The house package arrives at your site via tractor-trailer with all the parts labeled and numbered in sequence. You put the walls together with the interlocking joints and the glue, one on top of the other, sealing the wall courses with glue as you go. Once you've built them, you don't have to do anything else to the walls—they don't need to be painted, and they're already insulated."

Designing a home with IHC is an easy task. The company provides a wide vari-

ety of stock home plans, but many people prefer to design their own. As Robin puts it, "People start out with a bunch of details that cohere into a house that's just for them. Most people start off wanting a wood house that's a little bit out of the ordinary. They take a look at the stock plans, and they usually end up with a heavily modified stock exterior, and they redo the interiors to suit themselves. Stock designs serve to get people thinking— they come in very handy for that. With IHC, people like to design open-plan homes with cathedral ceilings and loft spaces. This is an energy-efficient type of design that appeals to a lot of people—it's open and airy and very spacious. Everybody I've built for loves their home."

Debbie Woods of Rayland, Ohio, describes the process of designing her home. "We had always wanted a cedar home. We went to look at the IHC model home nearby and really fell in love with it. Our home is a chalet-style—an A-frame, laid out like a small ranch

Homeowners can design their own interiors for a custom look.

A gambrel roof distinguishes this Country Series home.

house downstairs with a loft bedroom above. It's about twelve hundred square feet. Our IHC dealer showed us the stock plans, and we picked something that was similar to what we wanted, and made some changes. Then they sent us the preliminary plans. We made the changes we wanted, and checked to make sure it was okay. It helped that we had a very clear idea of how we wanted our home to be."

The stock designs from IHC are easily adapted to different styles of living. The Alpine series offers lots of windows in combination with open living areas and loft spaces, in sizes ranging from 972 square feet to 2,718 square feet. The Leisure series includes smaller homes that measure between 272 square feet and 945 square feet, suitable as starter homes, homes for couples with grown children, and as vacation hideaways. Other design series feature a variety of both contemporary and traditional interiors and exteriors, including western-style homes and houses designed for relaxed country living. The largest standard design available is 2,718 square feet, although IHC will design custom-built homes of any size. These houses can be built anywhere—IHC even supplies special component packages for arctic and tropical climates. The prices for standard packages range from $10,037 for a 272-square-foot vacation home that employs standard 4 × 8 cedar or deluxe 5 × 8 pine, to $78,777 for a majestic 2,878-square-foot Alpine home. The price of kits increases according to the size of the timbers desired, so that a deluxe cedar 5 × 8 wall home, or one with 6 × 8 Thermo-Lam timbers, can cost up to $100,000 for the kit alone, not including labor. ∎

Here's what comes in an IHC kit:

- 2 × 10 floor beams, with treated mud sills
- Subfloor of ¾-inch plywood, and loft floors of 2 × 6 tongue and groove decking, with ½-inch particle board overlayment
- Roof system with finished ceiling of tongue and groove decking, 2-inch rigid foam insulation, 15-lb. roofing felt, 30-lb. shake liner and hand-split cedar shakes
- Interior and exterior cedar trim
- Double-glazed insulated bronzetone aluminum frame sliding windows and sliding glass doors (wood insulated windows optional)
- Flush mahogany pre-hung interior doors, with hardware
- Solid core, flush mahogany pre-hung exterior doors, with hardware
- All nails, caulking, adhesive, and flashing

Top: A modified version of the Belaire, a design well-suited to sloping sites.

Bottom: Home from the Alpine Series features a dramatic sloping roof.

LODGE LOGS

Lodge Logs manufactures truss systems and log walls, engineered with pre-cut window and door openings, pre-notched corners, and pre-drilled bolt holes. The logs, which meet FHA requirements, include curing curfs (cuts into the logs) to allow for even curing and relieve stress while curing. In addition to the standard wall and truss systems, Lodge Logs can also supply windows, exterior doors, and studding for interior partitions.

Multiple roof slopes distinguish a striking contemporary custom home by Lodge Logs.

The company's catalog offers numerous standard designs, as well as sketches of ideas for custom homes. Both standard and custom houses can incorporate any of the five log sizes sold by the company. Lodge Logs mills logs ranging from 6 inches to 10 inches in diameter and they base the prices of their kits on the thickness of the logs used.

Lodge Logs kits come with detailed blueprints and instruction manuals that provide step-by-step guidance through the building process. For an experienced builder, building any Lodge Logs home proves easy, but for the novice owner-contractor, the company offers the specially designed 768-square-foot Crafts-

Standard Floor Plan

The layout of a three-bedroom home offers a master bedroom suite and a separate dining room.

man. The more complicated Timberline and Pinedale models offer more space and more features. The Pinedale, for instance, has 2,516 square feet of interior space (with the optional daylight basement), and comes with one of two roof options and up to 5 bedrooms.

For those preferring a less traditional log home, Lodge Logs offers the 1,520-square-foot Cabarton, which features a contemporary exterior and a five-sided living room with a corner fireplace and a vaulted ceiling. The flexible design permits the substitution of a family room

for the nook and one bedroom, or the choice of a loft option that adds three bedrooms.

Lodge Logs also sells Kabin Kits, three standard mass-produced log cabin models ideal as vacation retreats or small, simple homes. Customers can only slightly modify the floorplans of the Kabin Kits, and may not make any exterior changes at all, but the three models are designed to meet a variety of needs. These packages include all the materials needed to construct a weather-tight shell ready for interior finishing.

Prices for Lodge Logs vary according to the model and the size of log used, starting at a low of $9,985 for a Craftsman basic shell and ranging up to $25,700 for a 2,017-square-foot Lakewood contemporary with 10-inch logs. These prices include only the wall and truss systems.

Standard Lodge Logs packages include all materials needed to build the log wall system: bolts, couplers, nuts, washers, key blocks, and fiberglass sealer. ∎

A beamed ceiling and massive fieldstone fireplace create architectural drama.

Many Lodge Logs designs include front porches.

NATIONAL LOG CONSTRUCTION COMPANY

The National Log Construction Company uses the Air Lock log system in its homes. The hollow cores of the logs make them easy to handle during construction, less expensive to ship, and much easier to wire for electrical service than conventional solid logs. National harvests its logs from the lodgepole pine forests that surround its plant in the Montana mountains.

Because it gives its customers a great deal of flexibility in selecting features for their homes, the company does not manufacture its homes on a production line basis. Prospective homebuyers send National a rough sketch of the house they want, showing outside dimensions and interior layout; the location of interior log partitions, windows, doors, and fireplaces; the types and heights of ceilings; and roof pitch. National sends back a proposal that quotes a price for the home and specifies the full list of materials.

The contents of each National house package vary according to the requirements of customers' designs. In addition to the standard materials included in the package, customers can purchase finishing items such as windows, doors, roof

Top & bottom: National designs offer a variety of roof profiles.

The materials provided in a standard Air Lock log package from National include:

- Exterior Air Lock logs, pre-cut for all window and door openings
- Interior log walls
- Log gables
- Window and door frames, with half-log trim on both sides
- Solid pole rafters, flat on one side and coped to fit log wall
- Solid lathe-turned ridge and purlin logs, cut to fit gables
- Solid lathe-turned log collar ties and trusses
- Materials for exterior roofed porch
- Materials for interior lofts and balconies
- Caulking compound
- Log assembly plans, construction details, and instructions

Top & Middle: Hollow-core Air Lock logs make construction quick and easy.

Bottom: Cathedral ceilings and catwalks make for an airy interior.

lumber, and roof shakes. Alternatively, they can eliminate from their package any items they do not want.

When the home office receives the customer's signed copy of the package proposal, along with a 15 percent down payment, National prepares a schedule that guarantees production time and shipping date. Thirty days before actual cutting begins, the customer pays 50 percent of the balance due on the kit. The remaining balance falls due upon delivery of the package.

Prices for National Log homes range from $6,270 to $83,685 for the standard log packages. Most kits cost about $15,000 to $20,000. ∎

NEW ENGLAND LOG HOMES

We consider ourselves country people—we collect antiques, have country tastes, and we just felt that a log home went with our life-style," says Rhonda McClellan of Grove City, Pennsylvania. "We liked the house for its uniqueness. The logs in the walls are so much bigger than the ones in the other houses that we saw. They're 9 to 12 inches in diameter. The size of the logs is one of the features that drew us to New England Log Homes in the first place. Also, they hand-peel logs rather than machine them into uniformity. They have knots, bits of bark still clinging to them. Every log has its own special look."

Hand-peeled logs are one of three exterior choices from New England Log Homes.

New England Log Homes, Inc. (NELHI), a leading manufacturer of hand-peeled log homes, is based in Hamden, Connecticut. NELHI manufactures its log homes in one of four factories across the country: Great Barrington, Massachusetts; Houston, Missouri; Lawrenceville, Virginia; and Marysville, California. NELHI constructs its homes according to its Total Building System, a step-by-step procedure that results in a

Old fashioned accessories add a rustic look to a log home bedroom.

completely engineered living structure.

NELHI uses pine logs, from 7 to 14 inches in diameter, harvested from New England forests. It gives customers three types of logs to choose from: authentic hand-peeled logs, machine-planed Panelogs, and the Duolog, which combines both techniques.

The Panelog provides a cleaner, sleeker look while still highlighting the natural beauty of the wood. The log features a flat, machine-planed inner surface and a uniform, gently rounded exterior. The Duolog offers a hand-peeled outer surface and a smoothly planed interior. Purchasers can stain, paint, wallpaper, or cover with Sheetrock the interior surfaces of both the Duolog and the Panelog.

To seal its walls, the company uses custom-manufactured TotalSeal—an open-cell clastomeric rigid foam saturated with a water-resistant sealing material and coated on one side with a pressure-sensitive adhesive. Applied to the tongue of the log, it helps to keep a wall sealed tight. The foam also adjusts automatically to the settling process and comes with a ten-year warranty.

With the Total Building System and TotalSeal wall, NELHI offers the Total-Shield Roofing System. This roofing system comes in two versions: the Total-Shield I system, designed for use with a conventional wood truss roofing system, and the TotalShield II, used with the heavy timber rafter system. TotalShield I includes the trusses themselves, plywood underlayment, felt, and fiberglass shingles. TotalShield II offers an R-rating of almost 19. The fire-retardant fiberglass shingles, molded to resemble cedar shakes, come with a twenty-five-year warranty.

Beamed ceilings are a frequent interior feature from New England Log Homes.

Other special features from NELHI include double-glazed and insulated windows with tilt-out sash and removable grills for cleaning. A continuous cushion seal of weather stripping guards against air leakage, while the solid pine frame harmonizes with the rustic log exterior.

Many people choose to build their log homes themselves, while others employ a contractor. All NELHI package components receive numbers and codes to correspond with those in the building manual and on the blueprints, making instructions easy to follow. Some local NELHI dealers, who also do contracting, can provide building services with a log home package. "The local dealer built our home for us," says Goldie Thomas of

Bottom: Even the newest log home has an old-time look.

Moneta, Virginia, "and then we did all the electrical and plumbing work ourselves."

The McClellans, on the other hand, built their home themselves. "My husband is a teacher who does construction work in the summers to supplement our income," notes Rhonda. "He had those three months free to work on our house. It went up very quickly. We moved in when it was about ninety percent finished—not completely done, but done enough to live in. That took about three months. It was a very straightforward process."

NELHI offers a wide range of home models in two different types of construction: the Homestead series, offering log-wall first floors with conventional construction above, and the Authentic series, with complete log construction, including log second floors, gable ends, and roofs.

The Thomases, for instance, built a Cambridge A from the Homestead series. The Cambridge, a three-bedroom ranch, features a great room—a combination kitchen-living-dining room—with a picture window. The model comes in two sizes. The "A" version, 24' × 44', offers 1,056 square feet of living space; the 24' × 52' "B," 1,248 square feet. The model also has an optional cathedral ceiling.

With NELHI's custom design system,

164

the Thomases could make changes in their plan at no extra charge. "We added a half-bath, and took advantage of the optional cathedral ceiling," says Goldie. "We have a full basement, a fireplace, and a wood stove. My husband is putting in another bath in the basement. Making changes on the standard plan was very easy to do."

The McClellans selected a model from the Authentic series, and chose complete log construction. Their 1,504-square-foot New Englander model offers family living on two levels, with three bedrooms, two baths, a cathedral ceiling over the living room, and a great room across the front of the T-shaped plan. The cathedral ceiling exposes the heavy timber roof truss system.

NELHI has also developed a design series of passive solar log cabins, called the SunSeeker series, which uses an isolated-gain passive solar system. The SunSeeker also features many south-facing windows. According to Mitchell Watson, NELHI's Director of Engineer-

The Barrington is one of New England Log Homes' most popular models.

Bottom: Custom detailing adds excitement to this striking model.

A front porch is the perfect place for happy, relaxed country living.

ing and Architectural Services, a solar log home with this design system can generate 67 percent of its heating needs from solar energy alone. "A wood-burning stove can supply additional heat, and a back-up electrical heating system can be installed for emergencies," he adds.

Costs of NELHI homes vary according to model, type of package, and the roof system specified. The New Englander, the home bought by the McClellans, for example, costs $28,865 for the basic package, and $35,490 for the total package. Smaller homes from the Authentic series, such as the 768-square-foot Richmond, cost $16,520 to $20,640. Much larger homes, such as the 3,328-square

foot Timberwood, the largest standard design offered by NELHI, costs $46,520 for a basic package and $60,470 for a total package.

The Homestead series, priced lower, features conventional wood roof trusses rather than heavy timber construction. A Cambridge "A," such as that owned by the Thomases, comes to $13,150 as a basic package, and $15,925 for a complete package with the roofing system. The largest Homestead series model available, a two-story Chatham with a two-car garage, costs $27,900 and $35,750. ∎

The Total Log Package from New England Log Homes includes the following:

- ☐ All pre-cut tongue and groove logs for walls
- ☐ All pre-cut tongue and groove log gable ends
- ☐ All heavy timber porch posts, plates, and sills
- ☐ All pre-cut heavy timber second floor joists and girders, laminated second-floor girders, and heavy timber girder supports
- ☐ Pre-cut collar ties
- ☐ Standard roof design for 50-lb. live load
- ☐ All pre-cut, heavy timber rafters
- ☐ All insulated rafter windstops
- ☐ Heavy timber roof truss and hardware
- ☐ Heavy timber loadbearing ridge beams, laminated load-bearing ridge beams, ridge beam wedge, and heavy timber ridge beam supports
- ☐ Pre-cut log posts, plates, sills, rafters, and sheathing for a dormer with windows
- ☐ Log siding to cover subfloor ribbon
- ☐ TotalSeal gasket, hardboard-end groove splines, urethane caulking, 10-inch-long spikes

- ☐ All pre-cut rough window casings
- ☐ Pre-hung insulated glass picture window
- ☐ Pre-hung glass tilt-out windows
- ☐ All pre-cut rough door casings
- ☐ Pre-hung, fully weather-stripped wood exterior doors, with storm doors
- ☐ Insulated sliding glass door with screen
- ☐ Construction guide
- ☐ Four hours of on-site technical assistance
- ☐ Twenty-four-month guarantee against insect infestation from Terminix

Also included in the Total Log Package, but not in the Basic Log Package:

- ☐ Tongue and groove, kiln-dried second floor-decking, and roof decking
- ☐ 2-inch rigid foam board insulation
- ☐ Shingle underlayment
- ☐ Roofer's felt
- ☐ Wood-like fiberglass shakes with twenty-five-year warranty
- ☐ All pre-assembled conventional roof trusses
- ☐ Gable and sheathing material

NORTHEASTERN LOG HOMES

M aine-based Northeastern Log Homes manufactures more than forty different models of log homes, which it has shipped as far away as Japan and the Middle East. Customers buy directly from the company, rather than from franchisees or dealers, and receive home packages complete with high-quality, brand-name components like Andersen windows and Peachtree doors.

Harvested from the Maine forests, Northeastern's Eastern white pine logs work easily, take a fine finish, and dry predictably. The company ages the timbers for six months to a year before milling them to uniform sizes and treating them with preservative chemicals. Northeastern homes feature rounded log exteriors and interior walls milled flat. The v-notches milled into the interior surfaces of the log walls match the appearance of the knotty pine paneling used on interior partitions. Spruce beams—strong enough to handle exceptionally long spans—support the roof and lend a rustic air to interior decor.

Workers building a Northeastern home easily fit the custom cut, tongue and grooved logs together with ten-inch steel spikes, installing PVC foam gaskets and using caulking to seal the walls. The tight log walls serve as good insulators, while a double roof system—which incorporates rigid foam for a rating of R-24—insulated doors, and double-glazed windows with optional storm

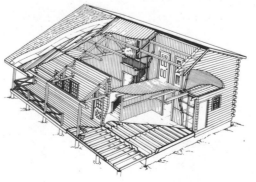

A cutaway drawing shows all the components of a standard materials package from Northeastern.

panels enhance energy efficiency even further. Northeastern's designers can adapt the company's standard plans to accomodate active or passive solar features.

Northeastern's staff will modify standard plans at no extra cost, or design original homes to customers' specifications. Customers can select a variety of exterior styles, from A-frames to colonials to ranches; and interior features like cathedral ceilings, fireplaces, and lofts. The company's most popular model, the Bedford, houses four bedrooms, a kitchen, dining room and living room in 1,570 square feet. The two-story home includes a fireplace and cathedral ceiling in the living room, and a covered front porch extending across the full length of the house. The standard Bedford package costs $31,625.

At 3,168 square feet, the Bristol represents Northeastern's largest—and most expensive—home. With five bedrooms, a living room, family room, dining room, kitchen, and attached 572-square-foot garage, the Bristol costs $66,355. At the opposite end of the spectrum, the $16,250 Eagle's Nest offers one bedroom, a combined living-kitchen area, and a covered front porch in 672 square feet. Three models—the New Bedford, the Phoenix, and the Sunburst—offer passive solar design for prices ranging from $29,745 to $36,360 for three or four bedrooms. ∎

A standard Northeastern package contains:

- □ **Floor system: sills, girders, double headers, joists, joist blocking, subflooring; and porch and deck joists, sills, headers, and flooring**
- □ **Walls and gables: Eastern white pine logs, splines, PVC foam gasket, caulking, corner pads, ten-inch steel spikes, window and door jambs; and log siding for frame skirting, dormers, and shed porch gables**
- □ **Interior partitions: framing and knotty pine tongue and groove board sheathing**
- □ **Ceilings: Spruce beam ceiling joists, two-inch random width flooring for loft areas, one-inch random width pine boards for other ceilings**
- □ **Roof system: trusses, purlins, decking, strapping, felt paper, drip edges, shingles, and gable roof porches**
- □ **Windows and doors: double-hung and casement windows, sliding glass doors, exterior doors, interior doors, closet doors, hardware, trim, and door frames**
- □ **Miscellaneous materials: basement stairs, loft stairs, porch posts, dormer sheathing, and railings, plus three sets preliminary plans, construction guide, and three sets working drawings**

The smooth interior surfaces of the logs look like wood paneling.

The Bingham offers four bedrooms and three bathrooms for the larger family.

NORTHERN PRODUCTS LOG HOMES

The A-frame roofline of the Oslo model offers an alternative to traditional log home design.

Northern Products Log Homes has built log home kits of Eastern white pine since 1968. The company offers twenty standard models and the free services of its design staff, which can customize a log home to fit customers' tastes and budget, as well as the requirements of local building codes and climates. Whenever it sells one of its log homes, the company plants 100 seedlings in the buyer's name to replace the trees used to build the house.

The 6 × 8 logs used in Northern Products packages come in two styles: Contemporary, milled flat on the interior surface and curved on the exterior (also available in 8 × 8 thickness); and Traditional, rounded on both the inside and the outside. Fitted together with a tongue and groove system and 10-inch spikes, Northern Products log walls feature PVC insulating gaskets in every joint, and caulking between every log to produce a watertight seal. The drip-edge cut of each log directs rain away from the seam.

Not only does Northern Products' thorough sealing system minimize the chance of moisture infiltration, it also makes the most of the natural energy efficiency of logs. For this reason, the company calls its system the Energylog system. The dark-tone coloring of Northern Products logs facilitates the absorption of heat from the sun into the massive walls, where it is stored and later radiated into the interior. To make sure that as much of that heat as possible stays inside, the company uses triple-glazed widows with special interlocking corners. Every

Natural stone complements the exposed wood.

168

Northern Products Home also has a double-insulated roof.

The company pre-cuts each house kit—including door and window openings—and numbers it according to the buyer's custom design. When delivered to the site, kits include almost everything needed to build a complete house. A company representative inventories the delivery to make sure everything is there. And although the Northern Products manufacturing and shipping process makes assembly easy, dealers provide whatever advice homeowners need during construction.

Northern Products houses range in style from colonials to saltboxes to split-level ranches to contemporaries, and feature a variety of roof profiles, including gambrel and A-frame. Balconies and sheltered porches, lofts and cathedral ceilings can give these log homes a feeling of airiness, while stone fireplaces, breakfast nooks, and kitchens designed as gathering places can add a rustic coziness. These houses can accommodate families of all sizes, and many models adapt easily to additions.

The 425-square-foot Trapper A with 6 × 8 Contemporary I–style logs, priced at $10,795, represents Northern Products' least expensive model, while the 4,829-square-foot Cromwell, constructed from 8 × 8 Contemporary II–style logs and featuring four bedrooms, two fireplaces, and maid's quarters, tops the price list at $137,849. 1,000-to 2,000-square-foot Northern Products houses generally run in the $30,000, $40,000, and $50,000 range. ∎

Each standard Northern Products Homes kit contains:

- 6 × 8 tongue and groove pre-cut and numbered Eastern white pine timber
- Butt-joint splines, PVC foam gaskets, caulking sealant, and applicators
- 10-inch spikes
- Window and door jambs of random length 2 × 4s
- Tongue and groove log siding for floor frame, skirting, dormers, and shed porch gables
- Triple-glazed, double-hung windows with screens and wooden snap-in 6-over-6 grilles
- Insulated, safety-glazed sliding glass doors with screens and hardware
- Tempered safety glass exterior doors with frame and hardware
- Raised-panel pine interior doors
- Full-louvered pine closet doors
- Door hardware, lock sets, and butt hinges
- Floor system of 2 × 6 or 2 × 8 sills; 2 × 8 or 2 × 10 girders; 2 × 8, 2 × 10, or 2 × 12 headers; 2 × 8, 2 × 10, or 2 × 12 floor joists; ⅝" CDX plywood subflooring; and 2 × 6 or 2 × 8 porch & deck flooring
- All interior framing and knotty pine panel
- 4 × 8 beam ceiling joists
- 2-inch V-groove flooring for loft areas or 1-inch V-groove pine for ceilings (when no loft area used)
- Complete double roof system, including: pre-cut timber trusses, roof purlins, rafters, 1-inch V-groove knotty pine ceiling boards, roof strapping, ½-inch CDX plywood roof sheathing, felt paper, and shingles
- Basement and loft stairs
- Porch posts
- Dormer sheathing
- Porch, deck, and balcony cross rails
- Exterior trim
- Construction plans and manual

A log interior offers many design options.

PAN ABODE CEDAR HOMES

The Cavalier makes use of ample deck space and a daylight basement.

S ince 1952, Pan Abode has manufactured custom timber homes that almost anyone can build. Pan Abode can modify any of its more than fifty standard home plans to suit the buyer, or its architects can design original homes. Constructed from naturally air-dried Western red cedar and finished with special sealers, the company's homes offer the beauty, durability, and passive solar benefits of cedar, as well as easy maintenance and resistance to shrinking, swelling, and warping.

Pan Abode gives customers a choice of three wall systems for their home—two timber and one frame. For temperate climates, the single timber wall comes in thicknesses of three or four inches, while for colder climates the double timber wall provides an insulating value of R-40. Most of the company's standard home designs are available as Framecraft homes—traditional frame structures with Western red cedar exterior siding and interior paneling. For added insulation, the company also offers the Pan Abode Energy Wall, a variation on the single timber wall that supplements the cedar's natural R value with rigid foam.

With solid timber exterior and interior walls, a Pan Abode home has tremendous mass. This mass, combined with cedar's cellular structure, makes these houses ideal passive solar homes. When positioned properly on a site to maximize south-facing window area, a timber house serves as an excellent storage medium for solar heat. The walls absorb the sun's energy during the day and radiate the heat throughout the house at night. All of Pan Abode's houses offer significant thermal benefits and minimize the amount of work required from heating and cooling systems. One of Pan Abode's models, the

The Schooner's striking prow front is a Pan Abode trademark.

Solar Cavalier, is designed specifically to take greatest advantage of timber's suitability for passive solar heating systems.

Pan Abode cuts every home to order—it does not sell packages of standard-length timbers. Specially milled in the company's factory, timbers and beams require no cutting at the construction site, and fit easily together because they are precision notched. Pre-framed windows and pre-hung doors further simplify construction, and Pan Abode provides a complete construction manual with each kit. Pan Abode designs its homes to go up without a hitch, enabling many of its customers to serve as their own general contractors in order to save money. For even greater convenience, Pan Abode will, at the customer's option, supply carpet, floor tile, cabinets, fireplaces, stoves, and mirrored closet doors.

The typical Pan Abode house features exposed beams and timber walls throughout, but buyers have the option of using standard frame walls to replace any of the non-loadbearing interior timber walls. Pan Abode customers have incorporated lofts, saunas, indoor swimming pools, wrap-around decks, and sunspaces into their homes, and have added interior features like wood spiral staircases and stone fireplaces.

Ranging from tiny 350-square-foot vacation cabins to elaborate 8,000-square-foot estates, Pan Abode houses can meet the needs of people with diverse life-styles. The four-bedroom Solar Cavalier, for example, includes a solarium and an arctic entryway to maximize solar efficiency, and is large enough to accommodate any active family. The houses in its one-story Islander series, with galley kitchens and combined living-dining areas, make ideal starter or retirement homes, while the Excalibur series, featuring cathedral-ceilinged living areas and multiple decks, represents Pan Abode's top of the line.

Prices for Pan Abode standard designs range from a low of $7,900 for a post and beam framed 350-square-foot Eagle's Nest to a high of $83,000 for a 2,625-square-foot Excalibur with Thermo-Break double timber walls. The 3,100-square-foot Solar Cavalier runs $80,000. Prices do not include design modifications, construction, or electrical, plumbing, or finishing work. ∎

Pan Abode includes the following materials in its standard building kits:

- □ Insulation
- □ First- and second-floor systems, including framing, sub-floor, decking, and underlayments
- □ Exterior walls and gables of custom-cut Western red cedar timbers, tongue and grooved with lock joint at corners
- □ Pre-hung cedar raised panel exterior doors and pre-hung oak hollow core interior doors
- □ Wood-framed insulated double-glazed windows and sliding glass doors
- □ Western red cedar custom-cut interior partitions
- □ Roof beams, roof decking, and gable trim
- □ Fiberglass composition shingles
- □ Decks and railings of cedar
- □ Nails, flashing, hardware, glue, weather stripping, caulking, and putty

A cedar interior creates a rich paneled effect.

REAL LOG HOMES

Jesse Ware founded Real Log Homes in 1963 when he built his first handcrafted log building in Hartland, Vermont. Since then, the company has manufactured over 14,000 log structures—homes, commercial structures, and outbuildings—in its five factories across the United States.

Real Log offers a patented log wall joinery system called the Interlock System. The system incorporates baffles and channels into each machine-peeled and chemically-treated log. This type of joint both aligns the logs and creates an air lock, or air expansion channel, that traps outside air. During construction, workers also add self-stick foam gasket tape and Locksplines—PVC strips inserted vertically on butt joints and corners—that further protect against air and moisture infiltration.

Real Log produces more than forty standard home designs in sizes ranging from 660 to 3,000 square feet. The houses come in a variety of building styles, including traditional log homes, ranches, chalets, and contemporaries. Customers can select one- or two-story models. They may also choose from a number of solar designs, and options such as dormers, skylights, and wings. If they wish, customers can work with the company's design staff to customize standard plans or create custom homes. The designers make sure that all Real Log houses meet the company's requirements for structural integrity, planning efficiency, and engineering economy.

Real Log's Solar Series combines the

natural efficiency of log walls with passive solar heating techniques. One such model, the Prescott, features a gambrel roof, an air lock entryway, and roof skylights in the cathedral ceiling. Its open-plan interior allows sun-warmed air to circulate throughout the house. Customers can add wood-burning stoves to the larger solar models for a source of extra warmth.

The company produces four non-solar product lines: the Gambrel Series, which features gambrel roofs; the Gable Series, made up of traditional log home designs; the Ranch Series, which offers smaller home options; and the Summit Series of contemporary homes.

A member of the Gambrel Series, the Plymouth, is Real Log's most popular model. The house comes in a 1,552-square-foot model and a 1,920-square-foot model, each of which buyers can expand using the company's standard extension packages. Both models feature three bedrooms, two baths, a central fireplace, and an open-plan downstairs with a combined living, dining and kitchen area.

Prices for log houses from Real Log start at $10,300 for the cozy Windham A and go as high as $39,900 for the spacious Wilmington. The smaller Plymouth model costs $20,100 for the basic kit. ■

A standard Real Log package contains:

- Exterior walls, with pre-cut and numbered logs
- Pre-hung doors and windows for the log walls
- Ten-inch steel spikes for securing the logs
- PVC Locksplines
- Foam gasket tape
- Solid timber girders and log joists
- Log rafters and 2 × 12 ridge beams
- Balcony railings
- Louvers
- 2 × 8 rafters, ridge beams, and collar ties
- Porch posts, sills, and plates
- Porch log rafter
- Roof system for gambrel roof
- Log gable ends
- Three sets of working blueprints
- Illustrated construction manual
- Four hours of on-site technical instruction for contractor or owner-builder

The log walls have interlocking corners for a tight, secure fit.

A traditional "cabin" look, from the Gable Series.

WARD LOG HOMES

W̲e had wanted to build a log house for years," said Jean Gerlach, who lives in a Ward log home in Manorville, Long Island. "At first we thought about building one as a summer place in upstate New York, but we didn't like the idea of leaving it unattended for most of the year. It's a nice house, really homey. We think it's a great house. The logs give a warm effect—the house is easy to maintain and cheery. It's basically a conventional home with log walls. A lot of people thought it was a big joke in the beginning. Nobody believed we could actually build a log home out on Long Island, rather than someplace upstate. But log houses are really homes like any other—you can live in them year-round."

Ward Log Homes, based in Houlton, Maine and established in 1923, is the oldest manufacturer of log homes and the first to offer them pre-cut. It sells

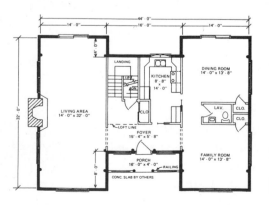

The layout of the Falmouth creates large recreational areas on the first floor.

only log homes built of Northern white cedar, chosen for its advantages as a structural material. It's light, works easily, shrinks very little, resists insect infestation and rot, and insulates very well. In fact, cedar has an insulating value twenty-one times that of concrete, eight and one-half times better than brick, and better than any other native American wood.

Ward selects only straight trees more than 100 years old and with a diameter of at least eight inches. Following its strict standards, the company uses only 28 percent of the wood it harvests as logs. The rest becomes dimensional lumber, paneling, trim items, etc.

After harvesting the cedar trees, Ward cuts the poles into 8-foot lengths, stacks them in piles in a yard, and air-dries the lumber for four to six months. Then it mills and grades the logs for use in walls.

"The biggest selling point with Ward," notes one customer, "was their use of cedar."

Josie Fletcher, a Ward dealer in Pelham, New Hampshire, who has built and lived in four Ward homes since 1962, says, "The big selling point with Ward, initially, was their use of cedar." Cedar has almost legendary resistance to decay and insects. In fact, tests have shown that an untreated cedar post lasts about sixteen years in the ground before succumbing

to rot, as opposed to only three weeks for untreated pine. Cedar also ages gracefully, weathering to a silvery color over time. However, some homeowners use a stain to alter the tone, or a clear preservative in order to maintain the natural reddish color.

The materials in a Ward kit show the company's attention to detail and quality—windows made of Andersen low-maintenance insulating glass, for example. Ward uses pine for pre-hung exterior doors, Colonial-style six-panel interior room doors, paneling for partitions, roof boards, and ceilings.

After sorting logs for use in the walls or other parts of the building, Ward precuts them to the proper length. Workers tongue and groove the logs and cut half-lap joints in the ends so that the logs fit tightly together. They also V-joint and sand each log to a flat inner surface and a

Ward offers many
different styles,
from traditional
to contemporary.

gently rounded exterior. The logs have extra caulking grooves and interlocking joints at the corners. Pole barn spikes eight inches long as well as caulking compound and foam-strip sealant, hold the log wall together and make it airtight. For accuracy, the company assembles the gable ends, cuts the proper roof slope, and then takes the gable apart for shipment to the building sight.

Ward cabins feature roof purlins — horizontal structural roof members that run parallel to the ridgepole, with vertical supports at the gable end. Regular rafters intersect the ridgepole at right angles. The company uses straight spruce logs for the purlins, which offer superior strength in long spans. The purlins make it possible to add practical and useful loft spaces in many of the company's models and allow customers to create cathedral ceilings that show off the massive roof beams. In addition to the purlin roofs, Ward offers an optional pre-as-

sembled conventional truss roof section, less expensive than an open-beam roof.

With well over thirty designs to choose from — and nearly 200 "standard" variations — Ward offers a flexibility in design. Its design department will draft any type of building compatible with Ward's construction methods.

"Our first house was a custom design," says Josie Fletcher. "The rest have been straight out of the catalog. Our current house is a Cape Cod style, with a story-and-a-half of living space."

The Gerlachs also chose a design out of the catalog and did not make many changes. "It is called the Liberty," says Jean. "It has a loft upstairs, a bath-and-a-half, a front porch, and a sun porch. We chose our house because we saw another like it several years ago that we liked. We had been interested in building a log home for many years. My husband can look at something on a page and know how it's going to be when it's built, but

Opposite page:

Top left: Horizontal purlin rafters support the roof.

Bottom left: The exposed inner structure makes for a rugged look.

Bottom right: The Bayview model has three bedrooms, a cathedral ceiling and a 292-square-foot deck.

me, I have to see the real thing. So we drove down to the model house. And when the time came that we decided to build our own house, we chose a very similar one. We made a few changes, which were very minor. We put a half-wall in between the kitchen and living room, instead of having it open, switched a few walls around, and asked to have a window put in where the fireplace was on the original plan."

Ward offers many different exterior styles, including a traditional Cape Cod home, a saltbox, a chalet, a split-level, a ranch, and others. It's easy to customize a Ward home simply by employing the standard options for a particular model. The houses can also sit on any type of a foundation, either a full basement, a concrete slab, a crawl space, or a post and pier type base, offering customers even greater variety when planning their homes.

In some models, builders can combine different types of roofs with various floor plans. Ward offers stylistic as well as structural options for roofs, including gambrels or roofs with steep pitches or a $5/12$ pitch (the roof rises five inches for every foot — a very gentle slope). The pur-

lin option can convert pitch or gambrel roof houses with lofts and upstairs living areas to single-story, ranch-type houses. The cathedral ceiling remains, but the loft becomes an attic. The $5/12$ option, when used with a truss system, creates conventional attic space and flat wood ceilings, eliminating the cathedral ceilings altogether. Gambrel or salt-box roofs always involve purlin-type construction.

All options affect the price of the kit. Substituting a double window for a sliding glass door, for example, reduces the price; adding an outswept roof overhang costs more.

Building a Ward home requires no special tools beyond those normally used for carpentry. The company labels pre-cut materials for easy on-site identification,

and pre-frames the roof purlins and tie beams to reduce construction time.

The Gerlachs chose to build their log home themselves. "We built the house little by little, payday to payday," says Jean. "We bought a shell-only package and did the interior little by little. That's one reason it took us so long—almost three years. You can really work at your own pace.

"We lived on the site in a pop-up camper for a while, and then moved into the house and lived there for a year, before we put in the interior partitions or any of the mechanical systems. We chose to do it this way because we had sold our other house and wanted to live on the property while we were building. We loved camping out. We would work from 4 p.m., when we got home from our day jobs, until dark, and full time on weekends. To begin, we each took six weeks vacation and worked full time on the house, starting with clearing the site and putting in the foundation. My husband built the foundation himself. It was

Country-style accessories help to create a homey interior.

Ward manufactures log garages in addition to homes.

the first time he'd ever done anything like that. A few friends would come by and help out some of the time, but we did most of the construction ourselves. It was quite an undertaking. We did our own interior finishing, too, and put up the wallpaper."

Ward furnishes log home kits in two versions—a shell-only package and a complete package. The shell for the 1,000-square-foot Innsbruck model costs $13,170. The complete package costs $23,230, and includes the floor, additional roofing materials, and interior components such as partitions, interior doors, and interior and exterior railings.

The Liberty model, such as that built by the Gerlachs, costs from $16,290 to $25,410 for a shell, depending on the options chosen, and $30,290 to $47,910 for complete packages.

Ward makes preliminary plans available for use in figuring costs and obtaining bids from builders. Standard plans require a $250 deposit, while the charge for custom plans comes to 2 percent of the quoted price. The company credits this fee toward the purchase price of home packages bought within twelve months of ordering the plans. Ward requires a 5 percent down payment before it begins manufacturing kit components.

Manufacture and delivery of a kit usually takes about four to eight weeks from the placement of the order. Buyers can request a particular delivery time, especially if it's not during the summer, Ward's busy season. The Gerlachs, for instance, ordered their home in May, but didn't want to take delivery until September, when they would be ready to begin working on it. ∎

Dormer windows and an attached garage distinguish this custom home from Ward.

A Ward Cabin Company shell package contains:

- Log walls and related materials of standard grade Northern white cedar, tongue and groove top and bottom, preservative-treated, numbered, and pre-cut to fit
- 8-inch pole barn spikes, caulking compound, foam gasket material, and caulking gun
- Purlin roof system: Eastern white spruce purlins, purlin support posts and false purlin posts, all necessary metal brackets and bolts
- Truss roof system: pre-assembled units
- Ceiling joists and beams pre-cut to fit, with spikes as required
- Andersen PermaShield Narroline windows, with double-pane insulated glass, frame, trim, and flashing
- Pre-hung, weatherstripped, pine exterior doors with flashing and trim, all hardware
- Tie beams and false tie beams for purlin roofs
- Beamed trusses for purlin roofs, with hardware
- Rustic loft stairs of Eastern white spruce
- Spruce or cedar support posts, with hardware
- Complete construction plans, and step-by-step construction manual

DOME HOMES

*B*uckminster Fuller, inventor, philosopher, and architect, developed the idea for using the geodesic dome for homes in the early 1950s. The triangular building block, the basis of dome construction, produces a stronger, more rigid, and more stress-resistant structure than that of more conventionally shaped homes. A dome's curved surface encloses *more* interior space while using *less* material and exposing less surface area to the elements than does a rectangular home. In the open interior of a dome, air flows freely, eliminating hot spots and allowing for simpler heating and ventilation systems. Owners save one third to one half on energy bills with these energy-efficient structures.

Revolutionary in the 1960s, today geodesic domes serve as homes to many people, most of whom built their house from a kit. "The mathematics are difficult to do from scratch," Blair Wolfram of the Daystar Shelter Corporation of Minneapolis, Minnesota says of the principle behind the geodesic dome. "But building from the kit is a picnic. Everything is color-coded and numbered, the struts are pre-cut, the bolt holes are pre-drilled, the windows are pre-mounted."

Manufacturers use two different mathematical principles to design domes, each resulting in a different structure. Fuller and his associates developed and franchised the Pease design, by far the most common dome design, in the 1950s. Pease domes use two sizes of triangles and have five natural openings around the base perimeter that owners can build onto for extensions. Homeowners can use the extensions simply to add floor space, or turn them into additional rooms. Most dome manufacturers supply extension kits, permitting homeowners to add everything from breakfast nooks to solar greenhouses.

By contrast, the Kruschke dome has a natural cut-off line and sits flat on the ground. This type of dome uses three sizes of triangles, and the frame can incorporate flat triangular windows on the ground floor for a panoramic view—a feature requiring extensions in a Pease dome.

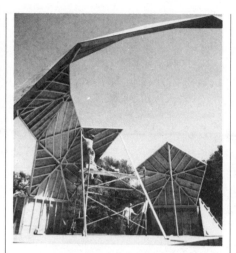

Manufacturers most commonly employ the hub-and-strut and panelized methods of construction for their dome kits. The hub-and-strut method uses two basic pieces to form the frame. A steel hexagonal hub holds the structural members (the struts) in place, and the whole framework goes up like a giant Tinkertoy. Builders then cover the frame with insulation and exterior sheathing. Construction takes a day and a half with a three-person crew.

The panelized method uses pre-built panels which bolt together to form the dome's shell. The panels come pre-insulated and pre-drilled. Constructing either type of dome requires about the same amount of time and the same number of people on the construction crew. The 30-pound panel units, although heavier and more difficult to lift than a hub-and-strut framework, reduce the number of construction steps.

Domes come in many different profiles and sizes. Depending on the height and diameter of the dome, it can have two levels of living space, or buyers can cluster together units of various sizes for larger homes. Typically, builders choose a low-profile dome with a riser wall to provide added height for the loft space.

Manufacturers express the size of the dome in terms of the diameter and the "truncator," the proportion of a sphere—such as ⅜, ½, or ⅝—that represents the dome. A ⅝ dome is taller and encloses more space than a ⅜ dome. In a low-profile dome with less than half a sphere, a Pease dome would have sixty triangles; the Kruschke, seventy-five triangles. Designers make domes larger by either using bigger triangles or by increasing their total number or "frequency." The higher the frequency, the more nearly spherical the dome becomes. The 25-frequency dome at the EPCOT center, for example, comes close to being a true ball.

Do-it-yourselfers, however, don't need mathematical expertise to build a dome house. And despite their lingering reputation from the 1960s as offbeat residences, today's dome homes incorporate high style into their efficient designs. ∎

CATHEDRALITE DOMES

At the Knoxville, Tennessee, World's Fair in 1982, Cathedralite built a model dome called the "Home of the Future." It impressed Ted Benefield, and he eventually decided to build his own. "I liked its unusual appearance and energy-efficient construction," he recalls. "It's not like a conventional home. It's really different. Really unusual. People driving by always stop to look at it."

According to the company—on whose Board of Directors Buckminster Fuller, the originator of the geodesic dome, served until his death in 1983—the very nature of the dome makes it suitable to the kit format. Customers can easily build the structures by bolting together triangular space frames. Since each piece has straight edges, builders do not have to contend with the problem of meshing curved surfaces.

Cathedralite makes the triangular panels from 1 grade plywood sheathing. The company nails and glues the plywood (for extra strength) over 2×4 and 2×6 studs of kiln-dried Douglas fir, precision-milled so that panels fit tightly with no gaps. Predrilled bolt holes make on-site construction assembly easy.

"I think the Cathedralite building method is probably the best available," says Ted. "I finally decided on a Cathedralite dome after I saw one under construction. I was impressed with the way it went up so quickly. The panels just bolt together, and there you are with a complete dome shell. The materials are very good quality as well, which was another feature I appreciated."

Some Cathedralite dealers also function as builders, and those who don't can offer

A shingled dome has a wraparound deck and a dormer window.

Opposite page: Dome interiors allow for the incorporation of many custom details.

182

help and advice on where to find a good contractor. Purchasers may need that assistance, since they could have difficulty finding a builder. Many builders look for easy projects, and if they've never built a dome before, they may not want to try. "When I decided to build my own dome," notes Ted, "I asked for bids and found that some builders just don't want to touch a dome. Others, though, think the whole project is really intriguing. I ended up being my own general contractor. Personally, I would recommend building your own dome, or at least being your own general contractor. You can save a

---

*W*ith *no loadbearing walls to worry about, dome homeowners can have just about any interior layout they want.*

---

lot of money this way. Most people want to be involved in construction at some level—it's a good experience. Even if you hire a framing crew, it's not that expensive, because the frame goes up in a day—that's it, you're done."

Homeowners can use any material used in a conventional home to finish the interior of a dome. "Finishing a dome can be a little bit more difficult," concedes Ted. "You have to prepare yourself beforehand and be ready to experiment a little. It's different from a conventional house. All the Sheetrock has to be cut

into triangles. But if you follow instructions, it's really not that difficult to do. Just cut it out according to the blueprints."

As an alternative to Sheetrock, Cathedralite offers pre-finished cedar interior panels with exposed beams that reveal the geometric structure of the dome. Other options include extensions, which increase the floor area and can also serve as entry vestibules or breakfast nooks. The extensions fit into the large trapezoidal wall areas at the base of the dome, and can have either pitched or flat roofs.

Cathedralite also sells tinted and dual-glazed skylights, available in triangular, pentagonal, and hexagonal shapes. The company warrants all skylights against leaks and gaps for five years. If they like, homeowners can add cupolas to replace the five panels that form the crest of the dome. With vertical walls and panes of glass all around the perimeter, cupolas bring light into the center of the dome and aid ventilation when opened. Dormers, installed inside a triangular panel, can create more headroom on the upper level. And models like the Vista Dome add a full-story riser wall to the base of the dome for additional interior space.

The company offers three different types of dome packages: the uninsulated shell, the insulated shell, and the pre-finished shell. Each package includes prefabricated triangles to form the dome shell, panels for the riser wall (since the domes do not sit flat on the ground, builders must use a riser wall to form the base), and other items specific to the design ordered.

Cathedralite uses the Pease geometry principle to make its domes. The most common dome shape built following this principle is the ⅜ sphere. Within each category, each dome, regardless of size, contains the same number of panels—only the dimensions of the panels change. Typically, Cathedralite dome packages contain sixty panels. The company also manufactures a half-sphere, or ⅘ dome, called the Rio. Because of the difference in geometry, this dome requires fewer panels than do the ⅜ domes—thirty-eight. This dome, smaller than most of the ⅜ profile domes, has more of a rounded shape because it includes a greater portion of the sphere's curve. The Rio has a 26-foot diameter, 425 square feet of interior space, and rises 13 feet in the center.

Door overhangs protect against bad weather in winter and block the sun in summer.

Opposite page: The pre-built dome panels go into place and bolt together quickly.

Many different room arrangements are possible within a dome.

The Horizon kit includes all the materials to build a ⅜ sphere, 50 feet in diameter, 21 feet high at the center, with 2,800 square feet. This dome comes only with a 2 × 6 wall framework. The package includes two skylights. The next step down in size, the Alta dome, has a diameter of 39 feet, 1,500 square feet of interior space, and rises 16½ feet at its center. Other dome packages in the ⅜ series include the 35-foot diameter, 1,250-square-foot Cuesta, and the 30-foot diameter, 900-square foot Del Mar.

Cathedralite also manufactures a Low Profile series of ¼ sphere domes. These packages contain forty-five prefabricated triangles, with an 8-foot high riser wall (riser walls for ⅜ and half-sphere domes range between 3 and 6 feet). These domes come in 43-, 39-, and 33-foot diameters. Another dome option available to customers is the Large Dome series,

consisting of domes with diameters of 60 to 120 feet, in all three profiles, from ¼ to ½ sphere. Cathedralite also manufactures dome garages.

The domes can have any interior arrangement desired, and the accessories packages can help accommodate a variety of floor plans. Dormers, for example,

Top: A large dome has an attached garage.

Bottom: Because domes are self-supporting, they can have lots of windows.

186

provide extra headroom and more space in the upper areas of the dome. Floor plans from the Cathedralite plan book suggest different ways of using accessories to fully exploit the unique aspects of dome living. The company's design service can also help customers create their own floor plan or modify one of Cathedralite's standard models. With no load-bearing walls to worry about in these self-supporting, free-span structures, homeowners can have just about any interior layout they want.

"My dome is 2,000 square feet, with an open-plan living area on the lower level," says Ted Benefield. "The living room, dining room, and kitchen are all one big room. Then, in a second-story loft, we have a master-bedroom-and-bath suite. There are two other bedrooms on the ground floor. It's a pretty big house."

Prices for the domes start at $6,390 for the 425-square foot Rio ½ dome uninsulated package. An insulated Rio package costs $8,790. A larger dome, such as the 2,800-square foot Horizon, a ⅜ dome, comes in three versions: insulated, uninsulated, and pre-finished, which cost $18,940, $26,310, and $36,460, respectively. Prices for the Low Profile Home Series range between $21,136 and $28,055 for pre-finished shells.

These prices do not include foundation material, roofing, doors, windows, cabinets, and finishing material; or plumbing, electrical, heating and cooling materials.

All Cathedralite domes carry a one-year warranty on materials and workmanship from the date of delivery. During the warranty period, Cathedralite will repair or replace the product or any defective parts without charge. ∎

A striking contemporary living room in a Cathedralite dome.

The contents of Cathedralite packages vary according to the specific dome. ⅜ sphere domes include:

- 60 prefabricated triangles in 2 × 6 or 2 × 4 framework
- Fifteen-panel riser walls
- Five beveled base plates
- Two skylights (depending on the model)
- Five sets of canopy weather guards
- Five sets of flashing for canopies
- Four sets of building plans
- Hardware for bolting triangles together
- Hardware for strapping tension nodes and riser wall

Materials for half-sphere domes consist of the contents of the ⅜ dome package, but include only thirty-eight prefabricated triangles in 2 × 4 or 2 × 6 framework. Low Profile dome packages come with forty-five triangular panels. With Vista Dome packages, Cathedralite includes the following materials to construct the lower wall:

- Prefabricated exterior wall framing and sheathing (2 × 4-inch construction)
- Prefabricated interior walls
- Pre-cut risers, stringers, and treads for stairway
- Joisting system and subfloor for upper level
- Uncut framing material for upper level walls and openings

DOME CREATIONS

For over a decade, Dome Creations has manufactured and sold geodesic dome home shells. The company believes its domes represent the most technologically sophisticated homes on the market today, both because of the advantages offered by geodesic domes and because of the manufacturer's own commitment to quality and price value.

A Dome Creations dome kit consists of pre-constructed rigid panels. This makes building very easy, because the construction crew doesn't have to frame and sheath the entire shell. Dome Creations also manufactures pre-fabricated trapezoidal wall units, which become vertical exterior walls that can accomodate doors and windows. The company will build these to order, incorporating any windows, doors, and siding that customers choose. With the pre-fabricated units, workers can raise and enclose a complete Dome Creations shell in one day.

Because of their shape, domes have better heat flow and less exposed wall surface area per square foot of interior space than box structures, so they don't lose as much heat. To take advantage of and supplement the dome's energy advantages, Dome Creations designs include an airspace under the entire first floor area of each dome. This "plenum chamber" manages air flow within the dome. Eliminating the need for duct work, the plenum system and floor vents provide equal air circulation and radiant heat distribution throughout the house. Fans serve as inexpensive supplements to the circulation generated by a heat pump. The combination of the dome shape and plenum system result in energy savings of 30–50% over conventional homes.

Customers can choose from eleven standard Dome Creations home designs and work with the company to make custom alterations. In addition, fifteen different dome sizes offer plenty of flexibilty in designing original dome homes. To help buyers make a choice with which they will be happy for a long time, Dome Creations has developed a series of three worksheets for use while planning a dome home. "Planning Your New Dome" addresses such issues as the amount of space needed, how much a customer can afford to spend, and whether customers should build their dome themselves or have Dome Creations build it for them. The "Land Feasibility Report" covers local planning and zoning regulations, utility availability, and plot evaluation. Free with the purchase of a planbook, "Designing Your New Dome" helps buyers decide on a floor plan and features for their home.

Among the options available with the purchase of a Dome Creations home are skylights, dormers, and cupolas. Riser walls can lift a dome off the ground and increase second-story floor area, and extensions can create foyers and alcoves or join two or more domes. To add to the energy efficiency of their dome, homeowners can use pre-insulated wall units with high R-factor foam. Alternatively, they can solarize their dome with a photovoltaic system. Dome Creations also sells All Weather Wood Foundations—panelized wall systems of specially treated wood that can replace concrete basements. The AWWF is inexpensive and easy to construct.

Dome Creations takes advantage of bulk purchasing, factory construction, and the cost efficiency of dome construction (domes require less material to yield greater interior square footage than conventional structures) to offer the lowest possible prices on its homes. The 26' diameter, 735-square-foot Chip model costs only $4,400 for the dome alone, and Dome Creations has found that most people can have a complete Chip built for under $20,000. At the high end of the Dome Creations price range, a 50' diameter, 2,900-square-foot Big Sort dome runs $12,700 for the shell alone, and can generally be completed for under $60,000. ∎

A Dome Creations package includes:

- Blueprints
- Dome panels of ½-inch structural CDX exterior or waferwood, glued and stapled to 2 × 4 or 2 × 6 members
- Canopies to overhang the trapezoidal openings in the dome
- One standard skylight, tinted or untinted
- Bolts and various hardware

Domes are so energy-efficient that they can be heated using only a woodstove.

GEODESIC DOMES, INC.

Martha Ericksen, who lives in a GDI dome home in the North Carolina hills near Asheville, has had an interest in domes for a long time. "We lived near the GDI factory in Michigan before we retired and moved down here," she says. "We were able to go to the factory and see how the domes were made. We like them for their energy efficiency and their appearance. I also like the fact that there are no interior bearing walls, so you can have any kind of interior room arrangement that you want. I'd build another of these houses. I love the openness, the feeling of space. And my closets are the envy of everyone who comes to visit. You see, when you make squared-off spaces in an essentially round area, you get lots of little odd-shaped spaces left over, which make great closets. Domes have terrific storage!"

Anne Cowan and her husband sought something out of the ordinary for their home in Milton, Florida. "We wanted something that not everybody else had," she notes. "We sent away for information from a lot of companies, but we were really intrigued by GDI. We are very happy to have dealt with them. They were very good."

Geodesic Domes, Inc., based in Davison, Michigan, is the oldest surviving company of those initially licensed to manufacture Buckminster Fuller

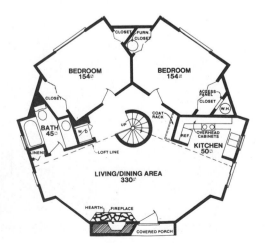

The ground floor of a two-bedroom plan.

190

domes. Family-owned GDI began in the 1950s, selling a single model—a 26-foot diameter Alpine dome. These days, GDI has two factories, and a network of dealers throughout the United States.

GDI makes kits for domes up to 50 feet in diameter. Purchasers can put them up themselves without cranes or other heavy equipment. The triangular space frames, panels with insulation built in, simply bolt together to form the wooden dome shell. Builders bolt two panels together to form a double-thick, double-strong frame. Assembly usually takes less than three days. GDI provides basic construction diagrams and describes building procedures. It also offers buyers detailed instructions for shingling, putting in drywall, and framing—somewhat different with dome construction than with conventional homes. These guides can also help subcontractors unfamiliar with dome construction.

The company's kits feature panels with pre-attached (glued and stapled) exterior sheathing and pre-drilled bolt holes. Each panel has a frame of 2 × 4 or 2 × 6 studs. The framing itself consists of kiln-dried, high-grade, stress-rated lumber secured with specially designed reinforcing metal clips. The company also includes temporary bracing lumber in the package.

GDI furnishes several factory-built options, among them riser wall panels;

extensions to fit the trapezoidal openings at the base of the dome and create additional floor space; both flat-top and Dutch dormers; and cupolas. Customers can incorporate passive solar heating and cooling into their homes with GDI solar greenhouses. The company also makes six different sizes of skylights, with double acrylic glazing and bronze-painted frames—each with a five year guarantee. The skylight shapes include a triangle (in four different sizes), a pentagon, and a hexagon.

Any room in a geodesic dome house can have a cathedral ceiling. Customers can also easily install lofts, open plan arrangements, spiral staircases, fireplaces, and balconies. GDI supplies several stock floor plans to choose from, or purchasers can design their own.

The flexibility of interior layout possible with domes initially attracted the Cowans. "My husband Tom designed our plan by taking two or three of GDI's stock plans and combining some of their features," says Anne. "Then he added a few flourishes of his own. He sent a

Top & bottom: GDI gives the homeowner many choices of interior design.

rough sketch off to GDI, and they drew up the working blueprints for a small fee. We designed it so that the second floor covers less than half of the full circle. Our living room is open all the way to the top of the dome, and we have a cupola at the top for additional light and to provide ventilation. After living in a dome, a conventional home is just too confining. Whenever we go to visit other people, we find ourselves moving outside, onto the deck or the lawn. We really love the spaciousness of the dome interior."

Martha Ericksen has lived in her dome since 1982. "We decided we wanted something really different for the inside. We knew that we wanted a cathedral ceiling and an open staircase. We have a long, curving open flight of steps up to the second floor. The staircase was a custom job, and had to be built on site. We did lots of nice things in the house. We designed it as our retirement home. In fact, because we have a sloping site, the dome is built into the hill with three of its five sides exposed on the lowest level. So we have a daylight basement, and in effect we're living in a three-story house. We've set up the first level, the ground-floor level, as a separate apartment in case we should ever become disabled. Everything is available on this floor, it's completely plumbed and wired, with a separate entrance."

With its catalog, GDI provides a floor

A soaring domed ceiling enhances spaciousness.

planning kit that shows prospective buyers several stock plans and offers advice on how to create interior plans. Using extensions and dormers, purchasers can create a variety of room layouts and increase the available square footage. Most of GDI's plans feature lots of open space, skylights, space-saving spiral staircases, and lofts useful for living or storage. The company provides extensions in various sizes, from 2 to 10

"After living in a dome, a conventional home is just too confining," says one owner. "We really love the spaciousness of the dome interior."

feet, with larger extensions big enough for separate rooms. Purchasers can also build domes in clusters to create larger homes and separate living zones. Some domes even have pentagonal wraparound decks. The domes sit on any type of foundation, from a crawl space to a full basement.

Customers can build their domes themselves or hire contractors to do it for them. "We hired someone to build our dome because we were still living in Michigan at the time. We had not retired yet," says Martha. "We got five sets of blueprints from GDI and sent them out to builders to get bids. We found out which builders had the best reputations from people who lived around here. Not one of the builders had ever built a dome before. One of them we never heard back from, and two of them declined to build it altogether. One said, 'I only build square houses!' Two were very interested. One submitted a very detailed proposal, the other just gave us a price per square foot. Their estimates were

Extensions and dormers make for different looks.

very close, but we went with the builder who had presented us with the more detailed one. We felt he had given it a lot more thoughtful consideration. The house became the talk of the county. People came from miles around to look at this house because at that time there weren't any other domes in this area, although now there are a few."

By contrast, the Cowans did their own general contracting and much of the labor on their dome. "My husband got his Florida contractor's license," reports Anne. "He hired a few guys who really knew about construction, but none of them had ever built a dome before. They just used what was between their ears, followed the blueprints, and built the

house. We started the house in July 1983 and moved in March of 1984. Construction, not counting the stops and starts, took about six months. Putting the shell itself up only took two days, with a five-person crew—not the same people both days, even. Building the dome was relatively easy. We didn't have to rebore a single hole. Everything was precision-machined and matched up perfectly."

The finishing process can take longer with a dome than with conventional housing, since most finishing products—shingles, drywall, etc.—are designed for use on flat, rather than curved surfaces.

"With a dome, the roof becomes the

A wraparound pentagonal deck is an option from GDI.

walls. There's no clear break," points out Anne. "It can be a little more difficult than with a regular house. There's certainly more potential for waste. We hired an inexperienced crew to install our drywall, and they didn't follow the blueprints. They just whacked around and ended up walking off the job. Those people didn't have the experience or the patience to do it right. It was a really unfortunate experience. My husband and son ended up completing the job, and they had no trouble."

"You have to go up on a scaffolding to put drywall on the ceiling," added Martha. "This is a little more difficult because you're working over your head, and that's hard for some people. But GDI supplies plans and instructions on how to cut out the drywall without making a big mess and wasting a lot of material. We had a builder do it, but I know a lot of people who did it themselves. Each piece

is cut and handled as an individual flat piece, so it's not like you're dealing with curved edges that are going to be hard to fit together."

Basic packages for GDI domes range from $7,500 for a 30-foot diameter $3/8$ dome with a 5-foot riser, to $12,000 for a 50-foot dome. Above 35 feet, riser walls cost extra, as do extensions, dormers, and cupolas. Spray-in insulation for the basic package also costs more. Replacing the 2×4 frame with a 2×6 frame adds about 20 percent to the price, and a $5/8$ dome costs 40 percent more for the basic package. ∎

A basic dome package from GDI consists of:

- ☐ Prefabricated triangular panels with 2×4 or 2×6-inch framing and attached sheathing
- ☐ Zinc-coated hardware, metal plates and straps, foundation bolts
- ☐ Five sets of canopies with overhangs
- ☐ Sill sealer
- ☐ Complete set of blueprints for dome assembly

A dining nook in an extension.

Traditional French doors look great in a dome.

MONTEREY DOMES

I wanted to build a dome for three reasons," says Gerald Befus of Winston-Salem, North Carolina. "A dome is energy-efficient, using a kit home meant I could be actively involved in the building process, and my house would be different from everybody else's house. I chose Monterey because I thought it was the best system for my situation. I didn't want to use modular construction, with prefab units that you just bolt together. The stick-by-stick construction meant that I personally could have a hand in determining the quality of construction, and I liked that."

Monterey Domes, a leading manufacturer of geodesic dome kits, uses a patented hub-and-strut building system, making shell construction simple even for an inexperienced builder. All package components come pre-cut, pre-drilled, and color-coded to minimize building mistakes. The color-coded framing lumber matches coded steel hubs where the triangles that form the dome shell converge. As long as the colors of the framing hubs and plywood triangles correspond during construction, the builder can't go wrong. After putting up the

A high-profile dome with cupola top, extensions, and attached garage.

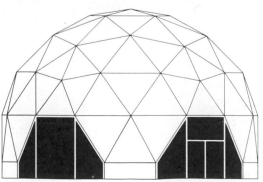

A drawing of a single high-profile dome shows its basic shape.

framing, the builder simply places the plywood skin on top.

Monterey uses 2×6 or 2×4 Douglas fir framing members for the dome framework, depending on the depth of insulation required. The larger 2×6 studs permit the customer to place more insulation in the walls. Construction requires only a few tools — a hammer, tape measure, pencil, level, ladders or scaffolding, box end wrench, socket drive, and crescent wrench. The building system saves money by eliminating the need to hire large construction crews to erect the framing. Homeowners do not need a crane, since the largest, heaviest piece in the package weighs only 31 pounds.

Walter Petty of Kokomo, Indiana, says of his experience building a Monterey dome house: "I investigated other dome companies besides Monterey, but the construction method and the high-quality materials appealed to me. I also

> "*M*onterey provided exemplary service," recalls a satisfied customer. "I give them absolute highest marks."

felt that it would be easier for us to build this type of dome ourselves."

Walter handled all the construction — except for the plumbing, electrical wiring, and furnace installation — right down to the crawl space foundation. "I

A dramatic interior from Monterey, with triangular skylights.

did all the drywall finishing and the trimwork myself," he remarks. "It was quite an experience. The whole thing went together just the way they said it would — like a giant Tinkertoy. We had the basic shell done in about a week, and then it took longer to close in the extensions. This was working as many hours as I could with a full-time job, so I was putting the dome up evenings and weekends. It went up pretty fast — and then we did the extensions, and the garage (we have a dome garage) so that took some time, too."

Gerald Befus had a similar experience. "I cleared the site myself," he says, "and I'm responsible for about 50 percent of the overall construction total. I subcontracted all the skill trades and worked with a carpenter on building the dome. I had never built anything before, not even a doghouse. In terms of how long it took, well, I general-contracted the project myself, while working full-

time, so there were gaps in construction—it wasn't a continuing process. Putting up the dome, from pouring the slab to close-in, took about three weeks. With four people working, you can get the basic skeleton up in about twelve hours. Plus I had five extensions to build, which adds to the amount of time it takes to get it finished—this is a big dome.

"Monterey provided most exemplary service," Befus adds. "I didn't ask for much help in the design, since I knew pretty much what I wanted, but as to the building part—well, I give them absolute highest marks. Their quality and customer service were great. They have a really good attitude. I was in constant contact with them after starting construction. I must have called them collect every day for four months, and they never failed to be gracious and reassuring, courteous and professional, giving practical as well as technical advice."

Monterey offers three design series and thirty-five standard plans, as well as a complete custom design service. Because of the dome's non-loadbearing interior walls, customers can easily mod-

ify the company's standard floor plans, placing walls and lofts anywhere.

The Alpine Series, usually built as two-family residences, have a high profile and vertical first-floor walls. They contain more interior space and head room than other designs. Each dome house in the series has ninety roof triangles and five ground-floor openings. They range in size from 1,040 to 2,627 square feet.

The Alpine 45, Monterey's largest standard single dome, comes in four standard interior arrangements, each 45 feet in diameter and just over 29 feet high. The largest standard plan, with 2,627 square feet, uses five extensions to create a home with four bedrooms, 3½ baths, a living room, dining room, kitchen, laundry room, and conversation pit. The semi-circular second-story loft features a central opening above the conversation pit and a balcony overlooking

Homeowners can use skylights, dormers, and extensions to customize their dome kits.

Opposite page: A skylight lights up a dining area.

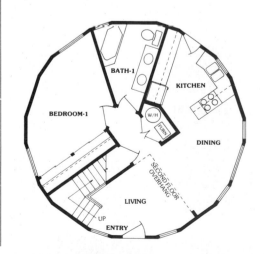

A suggested first-floor layout for one of Monterey's domes.

the living room and dining area. Dormer windows increase headroom in the bedrooms and in the master bath on the second story.

The Alpine Series 40 domes, in six standard plans, range from 1,959 to 2,176 square feet, and measure 39 feet in diameter and 27 feet, 4 inches high. The number of extensions and the size of the second-story loft determine square-footage and room size in each model.

Clusters—domes joined together to form larger homes—allow such luxurious features as a single small dome entirely devoted to a master bedroom suite.

Some extensions serve as large foyers, others as dining nooks or additional bathrooms.

The Horizon Series takes its name from its low profile. Each model has five ground-floor openings and sixty roof triangles. As in all its homes, Monterey designs the ground-floor openings to accept standard doors and windows as well as extension packages. The floor plans range from 290 to 2,138 square feet.

The largest Horizon Series model, the 45, encompasses a diameter of 44 feet and stands 21½ feet high. Customers can

With the hub and strut construction system, the framework goes up first, followed by the siding.

incorporate two bedrooms, 2½ baths, five extensions, a combined living-dining area that covers half of the first floor, several walk-in closets, and an enormous master bedroom suite on the second floor. Another, slightly larger plan has three bedrooms, 2½ baths, a family room in addition to the living room and dining room, and a laundry room. The house uses only three extensions.

The Horizon 40 features some ingenious variations on standard dome interior arrangements. In one model, measuring about 1,800 square feet, the second-story master bedroom sits on top of the central kitchen leaving a doughnut-shaped two-story space all the way around the exterior of the first floor—a reversal of the common practice of creating a central well. The plan, using five extensions, offers three bedrooms, 2½ baths, and several skylights. Monterey recommends the tiny Horizon 20, only 436 square feet with five extensions as a starter, vacation, or retirement home.

The cluster series consists of various domes joined together to create larger homes. Clusters make it relatively easy to add more space for a growing family. Clustered domes offer the greatest flexibility in designing interior areas, since purchasers can adjust the number and size of the domes as needed. Owners can vary dome heights by combining domes from the Alpine and Horizon series. The cluster method allows such luxurious

features as a single small dome entirely devoted to a master bedroom suite or a living/entertainment space. Children can have bedrooms in one part of the cluster, while parents enjoy privacy in another section.

Monterey customers enjoy a great deal of freedom in designing their own

homes. "I used one of Monterey's standard plans and altered it a little," remarks Gerald Befus. "It's easy to change it or add more space with extensions if you want to. We just changed a few things ourselves as we went along, it didn't require any kind of formal redrawing."

Walter Petty has the same feeling about the flexibility of Monterey designs. "We basically started out with a plan from the catalog," he says, "and then changed that one design quite a lot. We just did it ourselves as we went along. It was easy. We decided to eliminate one of the bedrooms, since we didn't really need more than three, and leave it as open space. We have a central kitchen, with a hexagonal second-story deck over it. We just left that open to a central skylight, although it was supposed to contain another bathroom."

Monterey offers several levels of finish. The Deluxe Dome Package contains all the pieces necessary for a finished dome, such as dormer packages, opening extensions, base walls, sky-

Domes of different sizes, clustered together, create additional living space.

The steel hub makes it all possible.

lights, and frame-in packages. Options include solar panel clusters, cupolas, a special roofing system designed to fit the dome, and canopy packages to protect windows and doors from the elements. Materials such as kiln-dried, stress-rated, structural grade Douglas fir for the framing members, and half-inch-thick exterior grade plywood for the skin, add to the structural integrity of each Monterey dome home.

Prices for Monterey domes vary according to the size of the home package and the number of options included. The largest standard dome plan, with 2,627 square feet, costs $22,625 for the deluxe dome package. The smallest dome, 436 square feet, costs $8,740. Cluster Domes, which include two or more attached domes, cost more. The largest standard Cluster Dome measures 3,851 square feet and costs $36,790. ∎

Two domes combine to form a spacious family home.

Each Monterey Domes Deluxe Domes package includes the following:

- ▫ **Three complete sets of endorsed standard construction plans**
- ▫ **Certified structural engineering drawings and calculations**
- ▫ **Assembly manuals**
- ▫ **Patented Douglas fir framing members**
- ▫ **Steel hubs**
- ▫ **Plywood triangles**
- ▫ **Opening extensions**
- ▫ **Canopy packages**
- ▫ **Base wall packages**
- ▫ **Dormer frame-in packages**
- ▫ **Skylights**
- ▫ **Skylight frame-in packages**
- ▫ **All fasteners and hardware**

Available options include:

- ▫ **Monterey roofing system**
- ▫ **Solar panel clusters**
- ▫ **Cupola**
- ▫ **Insulation**
- ▫ **Optional skylights**
- ▫ **Custom architectural plans**
- ▫ **Monterey Dome garage**

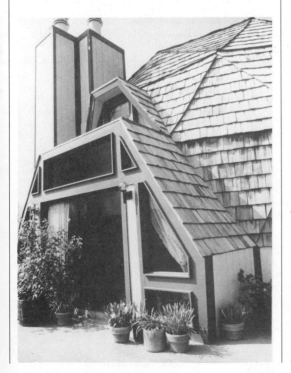

Entryway extensions also make good greenhouses.

STEEL-FRAME &
ALUMINUM HOMES

Metal house kits provide a sturdy, inexpensive, easy-to-build alternative to wood homes. Three American companies manufacture these kits: Tri-Steel Structures, based in Denton, Texas; Paragon Steel of Phoenix, Arizona; and Miami, Florida-based Endure-A-Lifetime Products. Tri-Steel and Paragon make steel-frame structures, while Endure-A-Lifetime produces homes of panelized aluminum.

Steel-frame homes have certain advantages over conventional wood-frame houses. They require fewer framing members, placed further apart—6 feet instead of 16 inches—because steel has greater structural strength. Steel-frame houses use less material, so they cost less than many wood-frame homes. And pre-cut steel frames, with all bolt-holes pre-drilled, go up quickly—it takes just five to eight days to complete a typical shell. In the words of Tri-Steel president John Brown, "The homes bolt together A-to-A and B-to-B, just like a giant erector set." The step-by-step construction process appeals to do-it-yourself builders, and makes it easy to add extensions to accomodate growing families.

Both Paragon and Tri-Steel use a 9-inch blanket of insulation in their home kits, giving walls and roofs an R-30 thermal resistance rating. This makes the houses relatively inexpensive to heat and cool—Tri-Steel claims

a savings of 60 percent on heating bills, compared with conventional homes of similar size. Steel-frame houses also adapt well to passive solar design, futher enhancing energy efficiency. The combination of solid steel framing and thick insulation provides effective soundproofing as well, greatly reducing the amount of street noise that penetrates to the interior of the house.

Stock designs for Tri-Steel and Paragon steel-frame homes range in size from 600 to 6,000 square feet, and vary widely in style. Both companies manufacture two basic types of homes: *slantwall* houses, which resemble ships' hulls turned upside-down; and *straightwall* houses, which look like traditional wood-frame homes. Both styles come in single- or multi-family designs. Buyers can alter the standard plans to suit their needs, and can customize their homes with a variety of additions and door and window options. They have a choice of exteriors as well: the steel sheathing supported by the frame can accept exterior siding of steel, aluminum, or wood.

The self-supporting walls of steel-frame homes make for extremely flexible interior planning—interior walls and exterior doors and windows can go just about anywhere. The ultimate open-plan homes, steel-frame houses can accommodate clear-span interiors of any length, and widths of up to thirty feet. Many owners incorporate cathedral ceilings to make the most of the airy spaciousness of their homes. In addition to the design advantages produced by steel's strength, these homes offer tremendous resistance to fire, high winds, and hurricanes, and have exteriors which require a minimum of maintenance.

Aluminum houses offer benefits similar to those provided by steel framing. Endure-A-Lifetime manufactures single-story panelized aluminum buildings for residential and commer-

cial use, and ships them all over the world. The laminated panels interlock at the edges for strong, rigid construction. The light-weight, resin-impregnated honeycomb cores of the panels provide insulation from both noise and extremes of temperature.

Endure-A-Lifetime finishes the interior sides of its panels with woodgrain vinyl-coated hardboard that gives the appearance of wood paneling. On the exteriors, the company embosses the aluminum with a stucco pattern and finishes it with paint or enamel. Available in standard widths from 16 to 32 feet, the houses offer a number of design options. For instance, Endure-A-Lifetime will interchange panels to put doors and windows wherever customers like. ■

GLOSSARY

All Weather Wood Foundation: A foundation system employing pressure-treated wooden sills, plates, studs, and underground plywood sheathing in place of conventional masonry or concrete.

Balustrade: A stair railing, including the posts, which are called balusters.

Baseboard: A piece of wood fastened to the base of a wall or partition to conceal gaps.

Batt: A fiberglass insulation blanket, usually eight feet long.

Beam: A horizontal structural member of a building frame.

Bearing wall: A wall that carries the weight of the floor or roof above.

Bevel: An edge cut at an angle.

Blocking: A piece of wood used as a strengthening member of framework.

Brace: A piece of material used as a diagonal support for framework.

Bridging: A small piece of material employed diagonally for support between floor joists.

Building paper: Heavy paper placed in walls or roofs to protect against moisture infiltration.

Building wrap: Sheets of material used on the frame of a house to prevent moisture infiltration.

Butt joint: A joint in which two pieces of lumber meet but do not overlap.

CAD: Computer-Assisted Design; the use of computers to draw up house plans.

Cantilever: A projecting structural member supported at one end only.

Carrying beam: Any structural member that supports some or all of the weight of a building.

Casement window: A window that opens outward on hinges.

Casing: The framing members of doors and windows.

Caulking: Material used to seal cracks or gaps in construction.

CDX: A grade of lumber use to cover the exterior of houses.

Chair rail: Wall molding at chair height around the perimeter of a room.

Chase: A groove cut into masonry, log walls, or through floors to accommodate pipes, wiring, or ducts.

Chinking: Material used to fill in cracks between log courses in a log house.

Cladding: Lumber used to cover the exterior of a house frame.

Clapboard: Overlapping horizontal exterior siding.

Clerestory window: A window placed high up on a wall just below the ceiling, or on any wall above the roofline.

Collar tie: A horizontal timber that connects two diagonal timbers, forming the third side of a triangle and reinforcing the structure of a double-pitched roof.

Coping: The decorative top edge of a masonry wall.

Corbel: A horizontal projection from an exterior wall.

Corner bead: A strip of wood or metal on the outer corner of a plastered wall.

Cornice: Horizontal ornamental molding at the top of a wall, or projecting under the overhang of a roof.

Cove lighting: A lighting fixture concealed behind a cornice or in a recess near the ceiling.

Crawl space: A foundation that forms a shallow space underneath a house and allows access to pipes and utilities.

Cupola: A small raised structure on top of a roof, with windows around its perimeter.

Curing curf: A small notch cut into a log to facilitate curing.

Decking: Lumber used to make a floor in a loft or on the second story of a building.

Dimensional lumber: Lumber defined by its size, such as 2×4 or 2×6.

Dormer: A projecting window on a sloping roof.

Double-glazed window: A window insulated by an airspace sealed between two panes of glass.

Double-hung window: A window with an upper and lower sash that slide over one another to open.

Double-pitched roof: A roof in which two slopes meet to form a peak.

Dovetail: A fan-shaped interlocking joint between two pieces of wood.

Drywall: see Sheetrock.

Eaves: Roof overhangs.

End-matched: Ends cut to fit each other.

Fascia: Flat trim used on a cornice.

Fill-type insulation: Insulating material blown into a wall space.

Flashing: Metal used at roof junctions and angles to protect against leaks.

Flue: The channel in a chimney through which smoke, steam, or fumes pass.

Flue lining: Metal or clay piping used to line a flue.

Footing: The concrete base of a foundation.

Foundation: The structure that supports a house, usually built underground.

Framing: Lumber which forms the basic structure of a house.

Fresh-air exchanger: A device that brings fresh air into a tightly sealed house and exhausts the stale air.

Gable: The triangular wall section at the end of a sloped roof.

Gambrel roof: A roof in which each slope has two pitches.

Gasket: A seal between members, which prevents air infiltration through the joints and seams of a house.

Geodesic dome: A structure which uses triangular panels to form a dome enclosure.

Girder: A member that provides a base of support for bearing walls.

Glazing: The glass of a window.

Ground water heat pump: A type of heating mechanism which uses differences in heat levels above and below ground to heat and circulate water.

Gusset: A strengthening brace or bracket.

Header: A piece of lumber used to support floor joists, or placed above windows and doors to bear the load of the floor or roof above.

Heat exchanger: A device which heats and cools a house by balancing the temperature above and below ground.

Heel: The end of a rafter that rests on top of a wall.

Hip: An angle formed by the meeting of two roof slopes.

Hipped roof: A roof with three or four, rather than two, sides that slope upward.

Hollow-core door: A door with an insulating air space inside.

Insulated-core door: A door with a panel of insulation inside.

Jamb: The upright portion of a door or window frame.

Joist: A parallel horizontal beam used to support a floor or ceiling.

Kiln drying: The artificial drying of lumber in large ovens.

King post: The middle member of a supporting roof truss.

Lally column: A steel tube used to support floor truss beams and girders.

Lap joint: A joint in which two pieces of wood overlap.

Lath: Slender strips of wood nailed to rafters or other frame members to anchor slate or plastering.

Ledger: A piece of wood used to support joists.

Lintel: A decorative element above a door or window, that also supports the weight of the wall above.

Lock joint: A rigid joint between two pieces of lumber.

Louver: A horizontally slatted opening.

Low-emissivity glass: Glass engineered to release less heat energy to the exterior atmosphere than conventional glass.

Millwork: Lumber shaped by machine for a specific purpose.

Mitered corner: Beveled ends or edges fit together to form a 90-degree at the corner.

Modular: Made up of standardized units or modules.

Molding: Decorative wood trim strips.

Moisture barrier: see Vapor barrier.

Mortise and tenon: An interlocking joint in which a slot or hole (mortise) cut into one piece of wood receives a projecting part (tenon) of another piece of wood.

Mullions: see Muntins.

Muntins: Strips of wood, metal, or plastic that divide window panes; also mullions.

Newel post: An ornamental post at a stair landing or at the bottom of a stair rail.

Non-bearing wall: Any wall that does not bear the weight of a roof or floors above.

Panel, electrical: A device which links a house's source of electricity to its wiring system and controls the flow of electricity.

Panelized: A construction technique in which house parts, usually the walls or roof, are pre-assembled in the factory and then erected on site.

Partition wall: A wall that divides interior space.

Pilaster: A projecting portion of a foundation wall, employed for support of framing members.

Pitch: The angle of the slope of a roof.

Plasterboard: see Sheetrock

Plate: The part of a wall frame that runs across the top or bottom, to which studs are nailed.

Plenum: An enclosed space that serves as a distribution area for heated or cooled air.

Post and beam: Framework that uses large members set further apart than those in a conventional stud wall.

Post foundation: A foundation that supports a house with wooden or concrete posts or piers sunk into the ground.

Pre-cut: Lumber cut to size in the factory before delivery.

Pre-framed: Lumber joined into a structural frame in the factory before delivery.

Pre-hung: A window or door suspended in its frame in the factory before delivery.

Pressure-treated: Lumber treated with preservatives under pressure in order to force the chemical solution into the cellular structure of the wood.

Purlin: A horizontal beam that supports rafters.

Radiant heating system: A system that employs coiled heating elements embedded in floors, walls, and ceilings.

Rafter: A structural member that runs from the ridgepole to the exterior wall.

Register: A grill which provides ventilation and heat circulation.

Ridge: The point at which two roof slopes intersect; the peak.

Ridgepole: A beam that runs along the ridge and provides support for the rafters.

Riser, stair: The vertical member that joins the treads of a stair step.

Riser wall: A ground-level vertical wall that provides additional interior headroom in a geodesic dome.

Roof prow: A projecting section at the peak of a roof that overhangs a gable.

Roof truss: A factory-built framework used to support a roof or floor.

Roofing felt: Tarpaper used under finish roofing to protect against moisture.

R-value: A term that expresses a material's resistance to heat; a higher R-value indicates greater insulating value.

Saddle-notch: A semicircular cutout used to interlock corners in a log wall.

Shakes: Wood shingles split by hand.

Sheathing: A layer of material that covers the frame of the house and supports finish roofing or siding.

Shed roof: A roof with a single slope, higher on one side than the other.

Sheetrock: Gypsum board used as an interior wall surface material; also drywall, plasterboard, or wallboard.

Shell: The exterior structure of the house, including the walls and roof.

Shingles: Small pieces of material nailed to roof sheathing so as to overlap each other and serve as finish roofing.

Shoe plate: Lumber used as the base for an interior wall.

Siding: Finish material used to cover the exterior of a house.

Sill: The horizontal piece of lumber at the base of a wall frame.

Slab: A concrete floor poured directly on the ground or on a bed of gravel.

Soffit: The undersides of the eaves of a house.

Solar energy system, active: A system in which photovoltaic cells store energy from the sun for use in operating a house's mechanical systems.

Solar heating system, direct gain: A system in which a house is oriented on its site to face towards the south in order to admit the sun's heat through windows on its south wall.

Solar heating system, isolated gain: A system in which the sun's heat is collected in a specially built room from which it disperses to the rest of the house.

Solar heating system, passive: A system in which a house is oriented on its site and designed so that the maximum amount of sunlight enters into the interior to provide warmth.

Spline: A thin strip of material set into the groove of logs in a log wall to seal out cold and align the logs against shifting.

Stickbuilt: Conventional on-site house construction using 2 × 4 stud framing.

Strapping: Small thin strips of lumber used on a wall to secure sheets of lumber in place.

Stressed-skin panel: A wall panel specially manufactured to use fewer framing members.

Stringer: A horizontal structural member used for support, or to connect vertical members.

Stud: A vertical structural member of a conventional wall frame, usually a 2 × 4.

Subfloor: Plywood surfacing that covers floor joists.

Thermal slab: A mass of dense material used to store the sun's heat in a passive solar house.

Tie: A horizontal piece of wood that supports two rafters where they meet the exterior wall.

Timber wall: A wall formed by horizontal courses of squared timbers.

T-joint: A joint in which the intersecting pieces form a T.

Tongue and groove: A joint in which a projecting ridge on one piece of lumber fits into a recessed groove cut into another.

Top plate: A piece of lumber that runs along the top of an interior partition.

Tyvek: The brand name of a type of sheet insulation made of polyolefin fibers, manufactured by DuPont.

Underlayment: A grade of plywood used for subflooring.

Vapor barrier: Treated material used to prevent moisture from passing into the interior of a wall; also moisture barrier.

Wainscotting: Material, usually wood or tile, used to finish the lower part of an interior wall.

Wall course: A horizontal row of logs or timbers which are laid on top of each other to form a wall.

Wallboard: see Sheetrock.

Weatherstripping: Material inserted around the edges of door and window openings to seal them against air infiltration. ■

209

INDEX OF MANUFACTURERS BY TYPE OF HOME

DOME HOME MANUFACTURERS

MIDWEST:

Baker Domes
A Division of R.M. Baker Company
P.O. Box 226
Wayzata, MN 55391
(612) 473-5183

Daystar Shelter Corp.
22509 Cedar Drive
Bethel, MN 55005
(612) 753-4981

Dome Kits International
Lakeshore Road
Reedsburg, WI 53959
(608) 524-4555

Domes America, Inc.
6345 West Joliet Road
Countryside, IL 60525
(312) 579-9400

Geodesic Domes Inc.
10290 Davison Road
Davison, MI 48423
(313) 653-2383

Highlight Homes
53 Canyon N.W.
Grand Rapids, MI 49504
(616) 454-7343

Natural Habitat Dome Company
Route 2, Box 314
County Trunk "S"
Plymouth, WI 53073
(414) 893-5308

Natural Spaces, Inc.
Route 3, Box 105
North Branch, MN 55056
(612) 674-4292

SOUTH:

Diamond Domes/Biosphere Corp.
8602 East Temple Terrace Highway,
  Unit 17C
Tampa, FL 33617
(813) 988-3220

Dome Enterprises
3405 Flagler Avenue
Key West, FL 33040
(305) 296-2096

Domiciles, Inc.
4020 Center Gate Boulevard
Sarasota, FL 33583
(813) 377-9460

Geodesic Domes & Homes
608 Highway 110 North
Whitehouse, TX 75791
(214) 839-7229

Key Dome Engineering, Inc.
P.O. Box 430253
South Miami, FL 33143
(305) 665-3541

Southwest Geodesics, Inc.
4801 Brentwood Stair Road, Suite 406
Fort Worth, TX 76103
(817) 451-8283

WEST:

Cathedralite
P.O. Box 2490
White City, OR 97503
(503) 826-7200

Dome Creations
1202 South Highland Drive
Las Vegas, NV 89102
(702) 387-6311

Dome Homes/Geodesic Services
P.O. Box 6548
Bellevue, WA 98008
(206) 453-9416

Geodesic Homes Manufacturing &
  Sales
P.O. Box 1675
Bailey, CO 80421
(303) 838-5345

Hexadome of America
P.O. Box 2351
La Mesa, CA 92041
(619) 440-0434

McCarty Engineering
703 Third Avenue
Longmont, CO 80501
(303) 772-7755

Monolithic Constructors, Inc.
3007 East Telford Road
Idaho Falls, ID 83401
(208) 529-0833

Monterey Domes
1760 Chicago Avenue
P.O. Box 55116
Riverside, CA 92517
(714) 684-2601

Natural Habitat Domes of Alaska
SRD 9021-Q
Palmer, AK 99645
(907) 745-5464

Oregon Dome, Inc.
3215 Meadow Lane
Eugene, OR 97402
(503) 689-3443

Polydome, Inc.
3804 Ray Street
San Diego, CA 92104
(619) 574-1400

Synapse Domes
P.O. Box 554
LAnder, WY 82520
(307) 332-5773

Timberline Geodesics Inc.
2015 Blake Street
Berkeley, CA 94704
(415) 849-4481

LOG HOME MANUFACTURERS

CANADA:

1867 Confederation Log Homes
P.O. Box 9
Bobcaygeon, Ontario
Canada K0M 1A0
(705) 738-4131

Cee-Der Log Buildings, Inc.
4100-6A Street NE
Calgary, Alberta
Canada T2E 4B1
(403) 277-8501

Four Seasons Log Homes
Parry Sound Industrial Park
P.O. Box 631
Parry Sound, Ontario
Canada P2A 2Z1
(705) 342-5211

Les Maisons d'Autrefois du Quebec
5500 Chemin Renaud
P.O. Box 55
Ste-Agathe-des-Monts, Quebec
Canada J8C 3A1
(819) 326-6604

Pan Abode International Ltd.
6311 Graybar Road
Richmond, British Columbia
Canada V6W 1H3
(604) 270-7891

MIDWEST:

American Log Homes
P.O. Box 535
Bourbon, MO 65441
(314) 732-5206

Beaver Log Homes
State Route 2, Box 175
Fredericktown, MO 63645
(314) 783-3317

Bellaire Log Homes
P.O. Box 398
Bellaire, MI 49615
(616) 533-8633

Cedar Forest Products
107 West Colden Street
Polo, IL 61604
(815) 946-3994

Cedar River Log Homes. Inc.
424A West Saginaw Highway
Grand Ledge, MI 48837
(517) 627-3676

Gastineau Log Homes
P.O. Box 184
New Bloomfield, MO 65063
(314) 896-5122

Greatwood Log Homes
P.O. Box 707
Elkhart Lake, WI 53020
(414) 876-3378
toll free (800) 558-5812
in WI (800) 242-1021

New Homestead Log Co.
Oakmoor One, Suite 210
4725 Merle Hay Road
Des Moines, IA 50322
(515) 276-1942

Northern Land & Lumber Co.
P.O. Box 291
Escanaba, MI 49829
(906) 786-8087

Rapid River Rustic Cedar Log Homes
9211 County 511 22.5 Road
Rapid River, MI 49878
(906) 474-6427

Town & Country Log Homes
4772 U.S. 131 South
Petoskey, MI 49770
(616) 347-4360

Wilderness Log Homes
Route 2
Plymouth, WI 53073
(414) 893-8416
toll free (800) 237-8564

Wisconsin Log Homes
P.O. Box 11005
Green Bay, WI 54307-1005
(414) 865-7081

NORTHEAST:
Allegany Log Homes
RR1, Box 132
Houghton, NY 14711
(716) 567-2583

Alta Industries Ltd.
P.O. Box 88
Halcottsville, NY 12438
(914) 586-3336

Beaver Mountain Log Homes, Inc.
RD 1, Box 32
Hancock, NY 13783
(607) 467-2251

Country Log Homes
Route 7, Box 158
Ashley Falls, MA 01222
(413) 229-8084

Green Mountain Log Homes
P.O. Box 190
Chester, VT 05068
(802) 875-2163

Kuhns Brothers Lumber Co., Inc.
RD #2, Box 406
Lewisburg, PA 17837
(717) 568-3181

Lincoln Logs, Ltd.
Riverside Drive
Chestertown, NY 12817
(518) 494-4777
toll free (800) 833-2461

Lok-N-Logs
RD #2, Box 212
Sherburne, NY 13460
(607) 674-4447

Maine Cedar Log Homes
Main Street
South Windham, VT 04082
(207) 892-8561

Mountaineer Log Homes
Boot Road, Box 251
Downington, PA 19335
(215) 873-0140

Natural Building Systems, Inc.
Crockett Log & Timber Homes
P.O. Box 387
Keene, NH 03431
(603) 352-4047

New England Log Homes, Inc.
P.O. Box 5427
2301 State Street
Hamden, CT 06518
(203) 562-9981

Northeastern Log Homes
P.O. Box 46
Kenduskeag, ME
(207) 884-7000

Northern Products Log Homes, Inc.
P.O. Box 616
Bomarc Road
Bangor, ME 04401
(207) 945-6413

Pioneer Log Homes
P.O. Box 267
Newport, NH 03773
(603) 863-1050

R&L Log Buildings, Inc.
RD #1, Shumway Hill Road
Guilford, NY 13780
(607) 764-8118

Real Log Homes
P.O. Box 202
Hartland, VT 05048
(802) 436-2123
toll free (800) REAL-LOG

Timber Log Homes, Inc.
Austin Drive, Box 300
Marlborough, CT 06447
(203) 295-9529
toll free (800) 533-5906

Ward Log Homes
P.O. Box 72
Houlton, ME 04730
(207) 532-6531
toll free (800) 341-1566

SOUTH:
All Seasons Log Homes
P.O. Box 381
Forest, MS 39074
(601) 469-1555

American Heritage Log Homes
P.O. Box 216
Maggie Valley, NC 28751
(704) 926-3411

American Lincoln Homes
P.O. Box 669
Brattleboro, NC 27809
(919) 977-2545

American Timber Frame Structures
P.O. Box 226
Kingston Springs, TN 37082
(615) 797-4140

Appalachian Log Structures
P.O. Box 614
Ripley, WV 25271
(304) 372-6410

B.K. Cypress Log Homes
P.O. Box 191
Bronson, FL 32621
(904) 486-2470

Brentwood Log Homes
P.O. Box 616
Brentwood, TN 27027
(615) 895-0720

Canadian Log Homes
Box 480, Highway 76
White Rock, SC 29177
(803) 781-6070

Cypress Log Homes
P.O. Box 5933
Rome, GA 30161
(404) 295-2154

Eureka Log Homes, Inc.
Berryville, AR 72616
(501) 423-3396
toll free (800) 643-8344

Hearthstone Builders, Inc.
Route 2, Box 434
Dandridge, TN 37738
(615) 397-9425

Heritage Log Homes
Box 610
Gatlinburg, TN 37738
(800) 251-0937

Honest Abe Log Homes
Route 1, Box 84
Moss, TN 38575
(615) 258-3648

Log & Timber Corporation
P.O. Box 177
Hillsborough, NC 27278
(919) 732-9286

Log Structures of the South
P.O. Box 276
Lake Monroe, FL 32747
(305) 831-5028

Old Timer Log Homes
C&S Enterprises Inc.
442 MetroPlex Drive, 105D
Nashville, TN 37064
(615) 832-6220

Otsego Cedar Log Homes
8066 Northpoint Boulevard, Suite 108
Winston-Salem, NC 27106
(919) 748-8087

Rich Mountain Log Homes
P.O. Box 95
Cove, AR 71937
(501) 387-2804

Rocky River Log Homes
P.O. Box 992
1411 Concord Avenue
Monroe, NC 28110
(704) 283-2166

Satterwhite Log Homes
Route 2, Box 256A
Longview, TX 75605
(214) 663-1729

Shawnee Log Homes
Route 1, Box 123
Elliston, VA 25087
(703) 268-2243

Smoky Gap Log Homes
P.O. Box 562
Dallas, NC 28034
toll free (800) 222-5647

Southern Cypress Log Homes
U.S. Highway 19 South
P.O. Box 209
Crystal River, FL 32629
(904) 795-0777

Southland Log Homes, Inc.
P.O. Box 1668
Irmo, SC 29063
(803) 781-5100
toll free (800) 845-3555
or (800) 322-8880

Stonemill Log Homes
7015 Stonemill Road
Knoxville, TN 37919
(615) 693-4833

Tennessee Log Buildings Inc.
P.O. Box 865
Athens, TN 37303
(615) 745-8993

WEST:

Air-Lock Log Company
P.O. Box 2506
Las Vegas, NM 87701
(505) 425-8888

Alpine Log Homes
P.O. Box 85
Victor, MT 59875
(406) 642-3451

Authentic Homes Corp.
P.O. Box 1288
Laramie, WY 82070
(307) 742-3786

Custom Log Homes
Drawer 226
Stevensville, MT 59870
(406) 777-5202

Glacier Log Homes
5560 Highway 93 South
Whitefish, MT 59937
(406) 862-3562

Grown in Oregon Log Homes
P.O. Box 7316
Bend, OR 97708
(503) 388-4312

Homestead Log Homes, Inc.
6301 Craterlake Highway
Central Point, OR 97502
(503) 826-6888

International Homes of Cedar
P.O. Box 268
Woodinville, WA 98072
(206) 668-8511

Lodge Logs
3200 Gowen Road
Boise, ID 83705
(208) 336-2450

Majestic Log Homes
P.O. Box 772
Fort Collins, CO 80522
(303) 224-4857

Model Log Homes
75777 Gallatin Road
Bozeman, MT 59715
(406) 763-4411

National Log Construction Company
P.O. Box 69
Thompson Falls, MT 59873
(406) 827-3521

Pan Abode Cedar Homes
4350 Lake Washington Boulevard North
Renton, WA 98056
(206) 255-8260

Rocky Mountain Log Homes
3353 Highway 93 South
Hamilton, MT 59840
(406) 363-5680

Rustics of Lindbergh Lake, Inc.
Route 2745
Condon, MT 59826
(406) 754-2222

Telemark Log Building
Chaffin Creek Road
Darby, MT
(406) 821-4602

Western Log Homes
5201 West 48th Street
Denver, CO 80212
(303) 455-0993

Wilderness Building Systems
178 West Oakland Avenue
Salt Lake City, UT 84115
(801) 466-6284

Yellowstone Log Homes
Route 4, Box 4004
Rigby, ID 83442
(208) 745-8110

METAL FRAME HOME MANUFACTURERS

SOUTH:

Endure A Lifetime Aluminum Products
Prebuilt Structures, Inc.
7500 NW 72nd Avenue
Miami, FL 33166
(305) 885-9901

Tri-Steel Structures
1400 Crescent
Denton, TX 76201
toll free (800) 433-5555
in Texas (817) 566-3000

WEST:

Paragon Steel
7065 West Allison
Chandler, AZ 85226
(602) 961-0777

POST & BEAM HOME MANUFACTURERS

CANADA:

Modulex, Inc.
2524 Hamel Boulevard
Quebec City, Quebec
Canada G1P 2J1
(418) 681-0133

Zarchikoff Construction Ltd.
642 First Street
P.O. Box 1748
Kamsack, Saskatchewan
Canada S0A 1S0
(306) 542-2145

MIDWEST:

American Timber House
Escanaba, MI 49829
(906) 786-4550

Futurama Homes
5332 NW 25th
Topeka, KS 66618
toll free (800) 443-4777

NORTHEAST:

Bow House, Inc.
92 Randall Road
Bolton, MA 01740
(617) 779-6464

Deck House
930 Main Street
Acton, MA 01740
(617) 259-9450

Green Mountain Homes
Royalton, VT 05068
(802) 875-2163

Habitat/American Barn
123 Elm Street
South Deerfield, MA 01373
(413) 665-4006

Maine Post & Beam Co.
Box 37, Route 1A
York Harbor, ME 03911
(207) 363-6060

Northern Energy Homes
P.O. Box 463
Norwich, VT 05055
(802) 649-6413

Sawmill River Post & Beam, Inc.
P.O. Box 359
Leverett, MA 01054
(413) 367-9969

Shelter-Kit Incorporated
P.O. Box 1
22 Mill Street
Tilton, NH 03276
(603) 934-4327

Timberpeg, Inc.
P.O. Box 1500
Claremont, NH 03743
(603) 542-7762

Yankee Barn Homes
Star Route 3, Box 2
Grantham, NH 03753
(603) 863-4545
toll free (800) 258-9786

SOUTH:

Cedardale Homes
P.O. Box 18606
Greensboro, NC 27419
(919) 854-1753

WEST:

Farwest Homes/West Coast Mills, Inc.
P.O. Box 480
887 NW State Avenue
Chehalis, WA 98532
(206) 748-3351
toll free (800) 752-0500

Lindal Cedar Homes, Inc.
P.O. Box 24426
Seattle, WA 98124
(206) 725-0900

Pacific Frontier Homes
P.O. Box 1247
Fort Bragg, CA 95437
(800) 822-6767

Rocky Mountain Post & Beam, Inc.
P.O. Box 308
Larkspur, CO 80118
(303) 681-2203

Rocky Mountain Timberworks
P.O. Box 2098
Glenwood Springs, CO 81602
(303) 945-1223

PANELIZED & MODULAR HOME MANUFACTURERS

CANADA:

Imperial Lumber Company Ltd.
R.R. #1
Winterburn, Alberta
Canada T0E 2N0
(403) 962-4663

Kainai Industries Ltd.
P.O. Box 150
Standoff, Alberta
Canada T0L 1Y0
(403) 737-3743

Kent Homes Ltd.
P.O. Box 10
Debert, Nova Scotia
Canada B0M 1G0
(902) 662-2685

Morewood Industries Ltd.
P.O. Box 10
Morewood, Ontario
Canada K0A 2R0
(613) 445-3133

National Homes Ltd.
P.O. Box 245
Abbotsford, British Columbia
Canada V2S 4N9
(604) 853-1195

Nelson Homes
P.O. Box 620
Lloydminster, Alberta
Canada S9V 0Y8
(403) 875-8811

North American Lumber Ltd.
205 Fort Street
Winnipeg, Manitoba
Canada R3C 1E3
(204) 942-8121

Prebuilt Structures Ltd.
423 Mt. Edward Road
P.O. Box 216
Charlottetown, Prince Edward Island
Canada C1A 7K4
(902) 892-8577

Royal Homes Ltd.
P.O. Box 370
Wingham, Ontario
Canada N0G 2W0
(519) 357-2606

Valhalla Homes Limited
355 John Street
Thornhill, Ontario
Canada L3T 5W5
(416) 225-6950

Viceroy Homes
30 Melford Drive
Scarborough, Ontario
Canada M1B 1Z4
(705) 738-4131

MIDWEST:

Active Homes Corporation
7938 South Van Dyke
Marlette, MI 48453
(517) 635-3532

Affordable Luxury Homes
Highway 224 West
P.O. Box 288
Markle, IN 46770
(219) 758-2141

All American Homes, Inc.
P.O. Box 451
Decator, IN 46733
(219) 724-9171

Bristye, Inc.
P.O. Box 429
Moberly, MO 65270
(816) 263-7600

Buerman Homes
Route #1, Box 14
Highway 23 West
Cold Springs, MN 56320
(612) 685-3633

Custom Made Homes
416 South Robinson Street
Bloomington, IL 61701
(309) 828-6261

Dynamic Homes
P.O. Box 1137
525 Roosevelt Avenue
Detroit Lakes, MN 56501
(218) 847-2611

Galaxy Homes, Inc.
P.O. Box 219
Dyersville, IA 52040
(319) 875-2421

General Housing Corporation
900 Andre Street
Bay City, MI 48706
(517) 684-8078

Home Manufacturing & Supply Co.
4401 East 6th Street
Sioux Falls, SD 57103
(605) 336-0730

Homes International
2201 Florida Avenue South
Minneapolis, MN 55426
(612) 542-4300

Kensett Homes
P.O. Box 157
Kensett, IA 50448
(515) 845-2201

Loch Homes
551 Packerland Drive
Green Bay, WI 54303
(414) 497-3550

Martin Homes
6901 West Old Shakopee Road
Bloomington, MN 55438
(612) 553-8300
toll free (800) 542-4700

Miles Homes
P.O. Box 9495
4700 Nathan Lane
Minneapolis, MN 55440
(612) 553-8300

National Homes Corporation
401 South Earl Avenue
Lafayette, IN 47904
(317) 448-2000

Pacific Buildings, Inc.
P.O. Drawer C
Marks, MS 38646
(601) 326-8104

Pease Company
Hamilton, OH 45023
(513) 867-3333

Permabilt Homes
Manufactured Homes, Inc.
330 South Kalamazoo Avenue
Marshal, MI 49068
(616) 781-2887

Permabilt of Illinois
Omnitech Systems, Inc.
P.O. Box 128
410 North Hemlock
LeRoy, IL 61752
(309) 962-2281

President Homes
4808 North Lilac Drive
Minneapolis, MN 55429
(612) 537-3622

Randall Company
Box 337
Piketon, OH 45661
(614) 289-4770

Standard Homes Co.
P.O. Box 1900
Olathe, KS 66061
(913) 782-4220

Terrace Homes
301 South Main
P.O. Box 1040
Adams, WI 53910
(608) 339-7888

Thermacraft Homes
Delta Industries
1951 Galaxie Street
Columbus, OH 43207
(614) 445-9634

Unibilt Industries, Inc.
P.O. Box 373
4671 Poplar Creek Road
Vandalia, OH 45377
(513) 890-7570

Wausau Homes, Inc.
P.O. Box 1204
Wausau, WI 54401
(715) 359-7272

Wick Building Systems
400 Walter Road
Mazomanie, WI 53560
(608) 795-2261

Windfield Homes
4700 Nathan Lane
Plymouth, MN 55442
(612) 553-8484

Wisconsin Homes
425 West McMillan
Marchfield, WI 54449
(715) 384-2161

NORTHEAST:

Acorn Structures
P.O. Box 250
Concord, MA 01742
(617) 369-4111

Adirondack Alternate Energy
Edinburg, NY 12134
(518) 863-4338

Advance Energy Technologies, Inc.
P.O. Box 387
Clifton Park, NY 12065
(518) 371-2140

American Dream Modular Homes, Inc.
225 Goodwin Street
Indian Orchard, MA 01151
(413) 543-4590

Barden Homes
Kelly Avenue
Middleport, NY 14105
(716) 735-3732

Coastal Structures Inc.
P.O. Box 2646
169 Pickett Street
South Portland, ME 04106-2646
(207) 767-3561

Contempri Homes, Inc.
Stauffer Industrial Park
Taylor, PA 18504
(717) 562-0110

Customized Structures, Inc.
P.O. Box 884
Plains Road
Claremont, NH 03743
(603) 543-1236

Epoch Corporation
P.O. Box 235
Pembroke, NH 03275
(603) 225-3907

Fairfield Homes
185 Thorpe Street
P.O. Box 400
Fairfield, CT 06430
(203) 259-8633

Green Island Homes
Center Street
P.O. Box 1538
Green Island, NY 12183
(516) 273-5473

Haven Homes, Inc.
RD Box 178
Beech Creek, PA 16822
(717) 962-2111

Hilton Lifetime Homes
36 Glenola Drive
P.O. Box 69
Leola, PA 17540
(717) 656-4181

Key-Loc Homes
P.O. Box 226
Suncook, NH 03275
(603) 485-7131

Marley Continental Homes
296 Daniel Webster Highway, South
Nashua, NH 03060
(603) 888-2191
toll free (800) 258-1888

Muncy Homes, Inc.
P.O. Box 325
Muncy, PA 17756
(717) 546-2261

Nanticoke Homes, Inc.
Box F, U.S. Route 13
Greenwood, DE 19950
(302) 349-4561

New England Homes, Inc.
Freemans Point
Portsmouth, NH 03801
(603) 436-8830

Nickerson Homes
15 Main Street
Orleans, MA 02653
(617) 255-2022

Northern Homes
51 Glenwood Avenue
Glens Falls, NY 12801
(518) 798-6007

Penn Lyon Homes, Inc.
RD #2
Selinsgrove, PA 17870
(717) 743-0111

Professional Building Systems, Inc.
Airport Industrial Park
Glens Falls, NY 12801
(518) 792-1048

Ryan Homes, Inc.
100 Ryan Court
Pittsburgh, PA 15205
(412) 276-8000

Techbuilt Homes, Inc.
585 State Road
P.O. Box 128
North Dartmouth, MA 02747
(617) 993-9944

SOUTH:

American Standard Homes
P.O. Box 4980
700 Commerce Court
Martinsville, VA 24115
(703) 638-3991

Arabi Homes, Inc.
Subsidiary of Flintstone Industries, Inc.
P.O. Box 117
Arabi, GA 31712
(912) 273-6050

Blue Ridge Homes
10620 Woodsboro Pike
Woodsboro, MD 21798
(301) 898-3200

Cardinal Industries, Inc.
P.O. Box U
Sanford, FL 32772
(305) 321-0220

Coker Builders, Inc.
P.O. Box 8
Turbeville, SC 29162
(803) 659-8585

Deltec Homes
P.O. Box 6931
Asheville, NC 22816
(800) 642-2508

Engineered Framing-Key-Kut
6201-B Dowdell Street
Fort Worth, TX 76110
(817) 429-6112

First Colony Homes
P.O. Box 224
Calverton, VA 22016
(703) 788-4222

Helikon Design Corporation
Cavetown, MD 21720
(301) 824-2254

Heritage Homes of Thomasville, Inc.
1100 National Highway
Thomasville, NC 27360
(919) 475-2171

Homecraft Corporation
Interstate I-85 and U.S. 58
South Hill, VA 23970
(804) 447-3186

Kingsberry Homes
A Division of the Boise Company
1725 Gault Avenue South
Fort Payne, AL 35967
(205) 845-3350

Mitchell Brothers Contractors, Inc.
Route 20, Box 500
Birmingham, AL 35214
(205) 798-2021

Mod-U-Kraf Homes, Inc.
P.O. Box 573
Rocky Mount, VA 24151
(703) 483-0291

Nationwide Homes, Inc.
P.O. Box 5511
Martinsville, VA 24115
(703) 632-7101

North American Housing Corporation
P.O. Box 145
Point of Rocks, MD 21777
(301) 948-8500

Northern Counties Lumber, Inc.
Route 50 West
P.O. Box 97
Upperville, VA 22176
(804) 592-3232

Ryland Building Systems
5585 Sterrett Place, Suite 100
Columbia, MD 21044
(301) 964-1173

Ryland Modular Homes
10221 Wincopin Circle
Columbia, MD 21044
(301) 964-6470

Summey Building Systems, Inc.
P.O. Box 497
Gastonia, NC 28034
(704) 922-7883

Topsider Homes
P.O. Box 849
Highway 601
Yadkinville, NC 27055
(919) 679-8846

WEST:

Andrews Building Systems, Inc.
225 South Price Road
Longmont, CO 80501
(303) 442-2562
(303) 772-3516

Armstrong Lumber Co., Inc.
2709 Auburn Way North
Auburn, WA 98002
(206) 833-6666

Cedarmark Homes
P.O. Box 4109
Belleview, WA 98099
(206) 454-3966

Custom Energy Homes
6990 South Jordan Road
Englewood, CO 80112
(303) 690-0880

Diamond Homes, Inc.
3279 South Santa Fe
P.O. Box 1716
Englewood, CO 80150
(303) 789-4451

Gentry Homes, Ltd.
94-539 Puahi Street
Waipahu, HI 96797
(808) 671-6411

Heritage Homes International
4850 Boxelder Street
Murray, UT 84107
(801) 261-5771

Independent Homes
P.O. Box 1030
Fairbanks, AK 99701
(907) 452-1826

Modular Homes
995 Commerce Circle
Wilsonville, OR 97070
(503) 682-2133

New Castle Homes
P.O. Box 108
9010 Main Street
Newcastle, CA 95658
(916) 663-3333

Pacific Modern Homes, Inc.
P.O. Box 670
9723 Railroad Street
Elk Grove, CA 95624
(916) 423-3150

True Value Homes
6425 East Thomas Road
Scottsdale, AZ 85251
(602) 947-7765

GEOGRAPHIC INDEX OF MANUFACTURERS

GEOGRAPHIC INDEX OF MANUFACTURERS

ALPHABETICAL INDEX OF MANUFACTURERS

PHOTO AND LINE ART CREDITS

The Preservation Press, from the book *Houses By Mail: A Guide to Houses from Sears, Roebuck and Company* (pp. 7–8); American Timber Homes, Inc. (pp. 3, 26–29); Henry Peach for Bow House Inc. (pp. 3, 30–37); Deck House, Acton, MA (pp. 24, 38–45); Green Mountain Homes, Inc., Royalton, VT (pp. 46–53); Lindal Cedar Homes, Inc., Seattle, WA (pp. 11, 25, 54–61); Northern Energy Homes, Norwich, VT (pp. 62–63); Pacific Frontier Homes (pp. 24, 25, 64–67); Saw Mill River Post & Beam Inc. (pp. 68–69); Shelter-Kit Incorporated (pp. 13, 25, 70–73); Timberpeg (pp.74–75), bottom photo on p. 75 by Richard Mandelkorn; Yankee Barn Homes, Grantham, NH (pp. 2, 76–83); Acorn Structures, Inc. (pp. 2, 86–93); Adirondack Alternate Energy (pp. 85, 94–101), insulation photos by Mark Antman (pp. 85 & 96); Affordable Luxury Homes Inc. (pp. 12, 15, 102–109); West Coast Mills, Inc., Farwest Homes Division (pp.85, 110–111); Continental Homes of New England (pp.2, 84, 112–119); Miles Homes (pp. 84, 120–121); Northern Homes (pp. 84, 122–123); Pacific Modern Homes, Inc., Elk Grove, CA (pp. 124–125); Topsider Homes, Inc. (pp. 126–127); Appalachian Log Structures, Inc. (pp. 132, 134–141); Berry' Beaver Log Homes (pp. 142–143); Cedar Forest Products Co. (pp. 144–145); Gastineau Log Homes, Inc. (pp. 146–147); Greatwood Log Homes, Inc. (pp. 3, 11, 148–151); Heritage Log Homes, Inc. (pp. 152–153); International Homes of Cedar, Inc. (pp. 154–157); Lodge Logs, Boise, ID (pp. 158–159); National Log Construction Company (pp. 132, 160–161); New England Log Homes, Inc., Hamden, CT (pp. 162–165); Northeastern Log Homes, Inc. (pp. 166–167); Northern Products Log Homes, Inc. of Bangor, ME and Statesville, NC (pp. 168–169); Pan Abode Cedar Homes, Inc. (pp. 170–171); Real Log Homes (pp. 133, 172–173); Ward Log Homes (pp. 14, 133, 174–179); Cathedralite, Inc. (pp. 180, 181, 182–187); Michael L. and Delores D. Provo for Dome Creations (pp. 188–189); Geodesic Domes, Inc. (pp. 190–195); Monterey Domes, Inc. (pp. 3, 13, 181, 196–203); Tri-Steel Structures, Inc. (pp. 204, 205); Paragon Steel Structures, Inc. (pp. 204, 205).